BRAIN FOG

Brain Fog

A true story of hope and recovery

N. J. Robinson

Moonshine Books Ltd
103 Shakespeare Ave
Bath BA2 4RQ

First published in Great Britain in 2024 by Moonshine Books

A CIP catalogue record for this book is available from the British Library.

Print ISBN: 978-1-7384742-1-9
E-book ISBN: 978-1-7384742-2-6

Printed and bound by CPI Group (UK) Ltd, Croydon, CR0 4YY

To Tom, Lily and Ella, who never gave up hope.

Preface

If someone had told me four years ago that I would be writing a memoir about health and healing, I would have likely laughed in disbelief. I was a busy, married, mum of two who didn't think twice about my health or what I put into my body. Besides a few gut issues, I considered myself robust and well.

Covid was a rude awakening.

I was felled by the original strain of the virus, the alpha, in March 2020. At that time, the world was still scrambling to understand what this virus was and how to treat it. Initially, I treated it like any other illness: I took some painkillers and headed to bed, waiting for recovery. I had no idea that the infection was just the beginning. I had no idea of what was to come.

The following chapters chronicle what would turn out to be the worst year of my life, but also the best. The worst for the strange, sometimes terrifying symptoms that ravaged my body and mind, and the best, for what this time of crisis ultimately gave me. When conventional medicine failed me, I was forced to look elsewhere. What I found rocked my world view, opened my mind and heart, and taught me the true meaning of health sovereignty. I finally learnt to stop outsourcing my wellbeing to others and reclaimed control of my own health.

The bitter irony of a chronic syndrome like Long Covid is that while it leaves you isolated, you find you are not alone. It is estimated that two million people suffer from Long Covid in the UK – but, as I discovered, Long Covid is only the latest in a range of syndromes that share similar complex symptom pictures. Myalgic Encephalitis (ME) and Chronic Fatigue Syndrome (CFS) are just two of these.

Published recovery rates for both ME and CFS vary; some estimate a recovery rate of 5%. This is alarmingly low. ME and CFS patients also have among the greatest levels of disability compared to other common diseases, with the lowest health-related quality of life score compared to cancer, diabetes, lupus, stroke, heart disease, and other chronic diseases.

The chronically ill are often too exhausted to fight their corner. In the past, they were accused of having yuppy flu; today, sufferers are often told they are mentally ill, or that they're merely having panic attacks. Sometimes they're plain gaslit – not just by medical professionals, but by close family members too.

This book is for all those suffering in silence with these misunderstood diseases. While this story offers a brief social history of the early days of the pandemic, it also seeks to paint a clear and honest picture of what it's like to live with a chronic disease like Long Covid. It also charts my own path to recovery: the people I saw, the therapies I tried, the diets, and so on. While I include the treatments and dietary changes that helped me, these do not constitute medical advice and are in no way prescriptive. I share this information in the hope that it inspires others to do their own research, just as I did, and find their own path to wellness.

Most of all, I hope this personal account offers hope that there *is* such a path. Recovery is possible and I am living proof of that.

This is a true story; some names have been changed to protect anonymity.

Chapter 1

Outbreak

It's the first of March and I am devouring as much media as I can. Scouring the headlines, repeated words jump out of the page and embed in my brain.

Grave, deadly, fatal, threat, risk, fear, surge, panic, outbreak.

They settle and make a home there, taking root.

I look up from my phone, out at the garden and a cloudy sky. So few planes… it's odd. Every new day seems impossibly far-fetched, as if a new reality is unfolding.

Tom joins me on the patio.

"Have you heard they're thinking of closing the schools?" I say. "I hope Lily's choir competition isn't cancelled, she's so looking forward to it."

"I'm sure it'll be ok," he replies. "We don't have many cases here, it's London that's bad."

"Did you hear about that GP surgery in Brighton? They had to close it all down for a deep clean." I swallow hard. "I'm worried about Dad." Dad, with his rheumatoid arthritis and immunosuppressants. Constantly in pain. Vulnerable.

"You've told him to stay home, right?"

I nod. Mum hadn't been keen when I'd urged her to start

getting food deliveries. *But I like my weekly trip to Morrisons,* she'd said. There's Mum getting to grips with staying home – and then there's my sister-in-law, getting to grips with so much more.

We're bracing as if we are on a war footing, she'd told me. *We've tried on our PPE, it's hot and sweaty and takes an age to get on, but we are ready.*

How brave our medics are, I think. Warriors.

That night I meet up with friends. We sip wine and talk about what's unfolding. About what's happening in Italy, about locking down.

"I'm stockpiling," says Lucy.

"Stockpiling what?"

"Oh, loo rolls and pasta mainly."

"But why? Isn't it a respiratory illness?" I'm perplexed.

Lucy shrugs. "Everyone else is. There was a woman online who bought eighteen loo rolls and found her kids had chucked them all in the bath. The whole bath became a soggy mush." She giggles into her wine.

"How will everyone work from home?" asks Kat. "Loads of people won't be able to do that. What about actors and chefs?"

"Trump says hundreds of thousands of people get better just by going to work," I say.

"He's a one-man biohazard himself," laughs Lucy. Then she shudders. "It's just weird. Like we're living in a film or something."

Back home I turn on the news.

The NHS has declared the escalating situation a level 4 emergency... Labour is challenging the Government on the lack of access to Covid tests… contain, delay, research, mitigate.

I understand the words but not their implication. New advice is to clean mobile phones as Coronavirus can stay on surfaces for up to a week. My hands feel clammy and my throat is dry; everything I touch might be contaminated. I make a note to stock up on more sanitiser and antibacterial wipes before work.

Next morning I stop by the corner shop. No wipes left, so I grab the last hand sanitiser. As I put it on the counter, I notice my hands. They're red raw and cracked from washing.

I head to the office before the others so I can sanitise the keyboards, monitors, mouses, toilet, taps, printer and door handles. A sense of overwhelm wells up: how can we possibly keep this place sterile? We can't. All we can do is hold back the tide. I force a smile as my colleagues wander in.

Then my phone pings. It's an update from BBC News.

Woman in China reports reinfection after initial recovery, others are still ill after three months.

My stomach churns and I can feel my shoulders tense. Adrenaline rushes through my arms.

Reinfection. The word binds to my subconscious.

Novel virus, ailing, diseased, sinister, contagion, incurable.

I bite my lip and try to concentrate.

We are a design studio with an international team and planes are being grounded. I send an email telling staff to book travel to their home countries now and not delay. Frantic searches ensue for seats to Madrid, Athens, Kuala Lumpur. I tell everyone to go home and pack and that we'll all start home working from next week.

We're an agile practice, we've often worked from home, we

can remote into our PCs from overseas if necessary. I tell myself it will be okay.

Later at the school gates, parents shift from foot to foot and nod in grim acceptance of what's unfurling elsewhere. I overhear snatches of conversations: "terrible… awful, those poor people, I had to turn off the news".

Lily comes bounding up with her usual wide-eyed grin, plaits bouncing off her shoulders.

"Mum, we watched Newsround and Mr Hartnett has told us about a big disease, he says we have to wash our hands and always sneeze into a tissue and do elbow high fives. Did you bring a snack?"

"Sorry love, I came straight from work."

"What?" Her face falls. "But you *always* forget. I'm starving!"

"I know, I'm sorry." I change the subject as we start walking home. "Are you ready for tomorrow then? All rehearsed and ready to go?"

But she's spied her friend and is already running to catch her up.

That evening, I find solace in the monotony and routine of chopping vegetables. I comfort myself with thoughts of a day off work and Lily's choir competition tomorrow.

I'm detached and absorbed over breakfast but force myself to be present for Lily as we leave for the concert. The community centre is already busy when we arrive. A grey-haired lady peers at paper stubs through her spectacles. I pass her my ticket and join other parents in the tightly packed chairs. Lily's a couple of rows ahead whispering through cupped hands to her friend Olivia and giggling excitedly.

I turn to a mum I recognise in the row and we get chatting. She tells me she's had to cancel a long-awaited trip to Italy for her wedding anniversary this weekend. It's becoming a familiar story – many people I know have had to cancel trips.

"With a bit of luck all this disruption will be short-lived," I say, hopefully.

A hush settles on the room as the host stands to introduce the proceedings.

As the first school of nine takes the stage, I think about how much I always enjoy watching the children sing. They're so energetic and hopeful, so full of life. Lily's class comes next. They carefully take the stage, mindful not to stumble or trip up the steps. Watching their teacher intently for his cue, they begin. They harmonise passionately – they're good, no doubt about it. I catch Lily's eye as she returns to her seat and give her a thumbs up, feeling a flutter of pride at her spirited performance. Applause fills the room.

Suddenly, something catches at the back of my throat. An urge to cough. The clapping masks the sound but the cough is there. *Strange*, I think… *like it came from nowhere.* But my throat isn't sore and I feel fine. I shrug it off: I know about the symptom of a continuous cough and it certainly wasn't that. I sip some water and await the next class.

Back home after school, Lily bursts through the front door.

"Dad! Dad! We got first and third place at the competition!" She's beaming with pride. "The cup has our school red ribbons on it!"

"Well done love, that's brilliant!" Tom picks her up and spins her around. "Have to get you on X Factor next."

"They did really well," I say, as we wash our hands. "Wow, I'm thirsty." I pour a tea, glad I've finished work for the week.

Days pass. I busy myself cleaning the house and responding to emails, but I've an uneasy feeling. I feel different somehow. I've noticed occasional twitching of my legs but put this down to nervous tension.

One day, I turn on the lunchtime news…

banks preparing for recession, many loved ones will die…

…my legs are flinching again. The sensation feels sinister.

That evening I find myself having to unhook my bra. My chest feels constricted, and I realise I'm drinking more water than normal for me. In fact, my thirst is insatiable.

Tom's on the sofa next to me, channel-hopping.

"Tom, I don't feel right," I say. "I've got no appetite and my mouth is so dry. I also feel like my hearing is off, which is weird. And my leg is twitching."

Tom puts the remote down and has a good look at me.

"I'm a bit worried I might have the virus," I continue. "I only coughed once, but I did cough last week. I think I'd better sleep in the box room tonight."

"Okay love," he says, and gives me a kiss. "They say for most people it's mild and you're fit and healthy. I'm sure you'll be fine in a couple of days."

"The kids can't go to school tomorrow," I say, walking up the stairs. "We need to self-isolate."

Up in the small, dingy room, the flinching in my legs turns to shaking and intensifies. I start to panic. I've got Covid, I know it. I think feverishly about what this means.

We must socially distance in the house. I can't see the kids, I can't see Tom in case I give it to him. Oh god, what if he already has it?

My mind reels with possible outcomes. If he gets it, we are both self-isolating. That leaves the children to fend for themselves. Ella's only thirteen but she can make pasta; they'll just have to look after themselves for a while. As for the grandparents, they're off limits.

What if they have to look after themselves for weeks? We could both die; they'd be orphaned!

My mind is spiralling into depths of despair. I admonish myself for catastrophizing and try to get practical.

What do I need? Paracetamol, thermometer, vitamin C maybe. Water. What else?

I have no idea what else. I want to antibacterial wipe the banisters but I'm too weak and my legs are shaking uncontrollably now. The rigours come in waves. I google rigours. 'A rigour is not serious in itself – however, some of the causes of rigours are serious and some need immediate treatment.'

Serious. Immediate treatment. Deadly, fatal, threat, infection.

I close my eyes. My temperature is rising and I'm clammy and cold. I clasp the thermometer and try to take the reading through sweat-stung eyes.

37.7. Is that in the normal range?

My heart starts to pound in my chest, sounding the alarm for the waves of terrifying chest tightening that follow. My breathing laboured, it feels as if the delicate branches of my lungs are being crushed from the inside. I'm drowning, suffocating, my chest hiding the sickening decay inside. In my feverish state, I'm glad I can't see the horror beneath my skin.

We've been told to stay at home, but how long for? Until I turn blue? Until I stop breathing or die?

This feels like madness, like succumbing. In a moment of lucidity I call 111. The nurse is patient and kind. She reassures me I'm in the peak of physical health and that I'll make a full recovery. It's a vanishing moment of hope followed by more malaise and despair.

As the illness progresses, day and night become increasingly blurred. Plates of food are left untouched behind the closed door. The cramped room feels musty and foetid and I start to hallucinate.

I'm in a shadowy garden overgrown with ivy and twisted thick brambles. In the distance I can see the dim outline of a bolted door. Stumbling through the thick undergrowth, I push against the jagged thorns that cut my face as I fight for the way out. I hear a murmur, a growing humming, a buzzing, louder, deafening. A swarm of murderous insects bursts from a vile, infested, bulging sack behind me. I run, stumbling and tripping towards the gate, desperate to reach the exit before they envelop me.

Rigours repeatedly signify the uncontrollable pounding of my heart and the constriction of my chest. I try to block the sound of ambulances carrying others into the night.

Am I dying?

I think of all the things I still want to do. I desperately want to see my children grow up. I imagine their weddings.

I just need a few more years.

I pray, and feel guilty for praying. But I desperately need salvation.

Does God exist? Will he help me? I'm forty-three, I'm not

ready to go yet. Please, I beg the silence.

As the darkness fades into morning, I feel the fever recede and the shaking stops.

I'm alive, I'm breathing, I think. *It's over.*

I could not have been more mistaken.

Chapter 2

Germ Warfare

For four days, the illness ravaged my body. By the third week in March, I felt able to get up – but I was very weak.

My weight had plummeted, my muscles were lank and toneless. My stomach burned after every morsel I ate. My lungs felt deeply diseased and I wondered if they would show signs of atrophy. My chest was leaden and my breathing raspy.

All that was bad enough. But what no one prepared me for, was what the illness had done to my mind.

I had lived an extremely sheltered life before Covid. I had heard of Ebola, SARS, HIV, malaria – but they were all exotic illnesses that happened thousands of miles away on other continents. I had never imagined we were at risk of infection in Britain. But as I saw it back then, the disease had evaded all detection: it had hidden in plain sight, boarded planes, crossed borders and attacked me in my hometown. This single-celled organism had been creeping unchecked, replicating through the community!

And so, I became driven by an urgent need to open all windows, clean the house, erase toxins and wipe out the dread I was feeling. Weak as I was, I wrenched myself out of bed, clutching the banisters to steady me to the bathroom. Grabbing the strongest cleaning products I could find, I began a frenetic, repeated sanitising of everywhere I had been.

I remember retching at the noxious fumes as I furiously scrubbed, and anyone crossing my path was subjected to unwarranted abuse. It was as though I needed to bleach out my trauma somehow. Gripped by this mania, I expended great amounts of energy that my body could ill afford to lose. Even just climbing the stairs was a struggle and had me gasping for breath. I had dyspnoea, an intense feeling of air hunger. Breath rapid and shallow, my chest felt heavy and compromised.

I should have stayed in bed, should have rested. But I had also developed a deep phobia of the box room. In my mind, it was a terrifying, dangerous place and I could not go near it. My rational mind was lost to me and all I could think about was pathogens. I had to eradicate them! And so I waged war, with my house as the battlefield. It was a lonely endeavour – no one in my household understood the urgency. I was in a state of high alert, my mind heightened to environmental threats. No matter how hard I scrubbed, how meticulously I disinfected, everything felt deeply unclean. When I finally stopped, it wasn't because I regained my senses, it was simply because life got in the way.

I considered myself well enough at that point to get back to work. And so, I did.

Perhaps a return to normality would have been the medicine my enervated mind needed. But when I emerged from that box room, I stepped into a world that was far from normal.

We were now in the first week of national lockdown. Having just hermetically sealed myself in for a week, I found the rest of the country had duly followed suit in an unprecedented act of civil obedience. Schools had shut, workplaces too, and everyone had been told to *Stay Home, Protect the NHS and Save Lives*.

My cleaning frenzy was quickly replaced by manically trying to work out how I was going to do my job remotely whilst simultaneously homeschooling two children. There was no question of Tom helping out – his workload didn't permit it – and so it had to be me. I would have to work part time and catch up in the evenings and at weekends. The girls would have to work... where? The only option was the kitchen table. I wondered vaguely if I'd find a spare table up in the loft. But it would have to wait; I didn't have the strength yet to go up there.

Homeschooling itself was extremely challenging. It was clear that I was not capable of teaching Key Stage Two Maths or English, no matter how much I hammered the search engines or tried to maintain the composure of a zen master. I went to primary school more than thirty years ago; I had no idea how to solve mathematical problems using the 'term to term rule', and I didn't know what a 'fronted adverbial' was. Did they even exist in the 1980s?

The entire family struggled in those early days. Tears were shed, tempers lost, and we argued about petty things. Raised voices would echo through the house, doors would slam during conference calls, the doorbell would trigger our unsettled dog into repeated barking. I was on high alert; a deep sense of unease haunted me morning until night.

As I watched the reality of the dystopian horror that was unfolding across Britain, I felt profoundly threatened. The news told us of many people suffering: ill, dying or in the throes of contracting the disease. Boris Johnson was in intensive care fighting for his life, Hancock and Whitty had both succumbed. The daily news took on a critical imperative reminiscent of the war years' *Dig for Victory* campaign. Everyone must help Britain win the battle. The Queen reassured us that "if we remain united and resolute, we will overcome it", but even Prince Charles had tested positive. The nation was now abiding by the two-metre rule as the global death toll approached 100,000 people. New messaging was telling the nation to *stay alert, control the virus, and save lives* but I was confused: how could I be alert to a threat I couldn't see? I had been hypervigilant and still caught Covid; how could I, an individual, control the virus?

Fear poured out from the news and into me. And yet, I couldn't look away. Instead, I hankered after any piece of news that might help me protect my family. The daily diet of death statistics and hospitalisations became like a drug fix for me. Reminiscent of the compulsive viewing of a slow-moving car crash, I continued to watch the devastation unfold.

Over the following weeks, we all adjusted haltingly to our new life indoors. Despite the challenges of enforced house arrest, I was glad for the space to recuperate without the pressures of the school run and commuting to work. I realised how manic my old life was and didn't miss it. Was this the new normal: working from home in perpetuity?

Slowly, very slowly, I felt my body begin to heal. I had to work very hard on breathing from my diaphragm; I was yawning and sighing more often than normal, and my breathing pattern was laboured and off key. My lungs felt leaden and heavy; I had never had access to a scan or any kind of Covid test and was glad I would never see the decay inside. I was managing gentle walks, but an impatient and ill-advised jog put me back in bed for days. My GP advised me to slow down, that I shouldn't have attempted a jog four weeks after a serious infection.

I spent what spare time and little stamina I had in the garden, trying to tame the rogue flower beds, my head bent under the unseasonable Spring heat. One afternoon, I set about uprooting some ivy that was inching unhindered through an impossibly small crack in the stone wall. I marvelled at the unstoppable force of the wild; nature always finds a way.

Satisfied, I stood back to inspect my work and my eyes rested on the broken wooden lattice on top of the wall.

I must fix that... that... the ...

What was the bloody thing called? I couldn't recall the word. I pulled out my phone from my jeans pocket and typed in 'wooden frame for climbing plant'. The answer came back: trellis.

What had happened to my mental recall? I was starting to forget words and occasionally couldn't finish my sentences. Just days before, I'd been to the toilet and instead of washing my hands afterwards, I had brushed my teeth. I had stopped and stared blankly into the mirror. *What the hell are you doing, you mad woman?* I said silently to my reflection. Other times I had put bread in the microwave to toast and inadvertently left the oven on. It would have been amusing, if it hadn't felt like a portent of a bleak outcome. My mind was not in a coherent state; something was misfiring.

Standing there in the garden, I tried to shrug it off.

It'll be all that multitasking I've been doing with work and the kids, I told myself.

I set about getting ready to paint the fence. I prised off the metal lid and stirred the gloopy grey mixture, watching transfixed as the undulations of the melancholy vortex uncovered lighter shades from its depths. Carrying the paint carefully down the steps from the back door I set the pot down on the grass. There were five panels to paint.

Shouldn't take more than two hours, I thought.

As I completed the third panel, heat was searing my neck and I started to feel dizzy. *Probably getting dehydrated*, I thought. I took a sip of water. Worryingly, fatigue was starting to creep in too, and my intuition was telling me to rest. I pressed on. I only had another hour until dinner and wanted to get it finished. By the time I got to the last panel, my heart was beginning to pound. I hurriedly put the paint pots away and sat down to rest.

By 9pm my symptoms had worsened. Beads of sweat formed on my temples. I had intense abdominal pain and in echoes of my initial acute infection, a wave of burning pressure coursed through my body. I panicked as my legs twitched and my heart began to pound, signalling the recurring violent convulsing of my legs that was to follow.

How had I caught Covid again? It was months since I had seen anyone. My symptoms were indistinguishable from before: the same rigours, temperature, hammering heart. I was truly terrified. My lungs were still ailing; they couldn't withstand more infection. I shouted anxiously to Tom as I headed to bed. Again, I thought about my children; this truly dreadful disease was going to rob me of my future. Why was this happening to me?

Lying prone, a ton of deadening, excruciating pressure coursed through my veins, sapping my strength and stealing the air from my lungs. While Tom fussed around me with water and paracetamol, I lay frozen, unable to speak, listen or respond. Finally, the inflammation subsided a little and I tried to think rationally. I would go to A&E alone – I wasn't going to risk dying at home with no medical intervention again. Lockdown laws meant Tom couldn't accompany me anyway, and there were the kids to think about. But, I was deeply confused. I had spent the last few months recovering, and now Covid had come back. How was this possible? I vaguely remembered malaria could stay in your system and then reactivate at intervals… did Covid do this?

Knowing the physiological signposts already made it emotionally more difficult to process, more alarming. To my horror, I was back in the dreary box room, reliving every moment of my previous acute illness as compound trauma. I knew at each point what would come next. The chilling familiar shaking, the fever, the pain, wondering if my heart would stop, the burning of my lungs in waves, repeat to fade. It was a mirror image of my original Covid experience.

The street was silent and dark when at 3am, I pulled into the space outside the house and set the gear into park. As I slowly swung my legs around and hauled myself out of the car, the gradient of the slope fought against me, swinging the door back and catching my skin. Wincing, I turned my key in the front door and walked slowly inside.

I knew the five-hour wait at A&E had been a good result, but I was exhausted and certainly wasn't well enough to have navigated the way to the hospital on my own – but there was no other option. The rules were that no one was accompanied to their medical appointments: I was fighting for survival, alone. The nurse had listened to my story and dutifully written notes; the same questions were asked again with the usual answers. It was tedious and energy-sapping. My ECG showed I was tachycardic, but as I lay in the hospital bed, wires attached all over my body, the doctor on call had approached to tell me I was fit to go home. I was incredulous. Why? I felt on the verge of my final breath, but this doctor was suggesting I had a secondary as yet undiagnosed infection, and would not be drawn further on the details. He must be wrong; I was sure I had Covid. My old symptoms had come back, so surely it was logical that I must have contracted the disease again, like that poor woman in China? Or maybe the virus was still in me and was flaring up again? I vowed to have a Covid test, now they were available. I just felt the medics were wrong, and felt deeply frustrated. I had been given no prophylactics, no treatment, no diagnosis and no prognosis. No one at the hospital knew what was wrong with me.

Go home and rest, the doctor had said. What else could I do? I took the drastic decision to stop all light exercise, reasoning that this would give me the best chance of recovery, but it rendered me completely housebound. I had been referred back to my GP for blood tests and despite my terrifying ordeal in A&E, I had full trust in the medical profession; I was confident they would find out what was wrong with me and give me the right treatment. The first of many calls to my surgery was about to begin.

Chapter 3

Insomnia

After that first relapse, my energy collapsed. Often, even the slightest exertion would set my heart racing. Suddenly, life became very small. I confined myself to the front room, staring out the window or watching TV, waiting to recover. I learnt energy shortcuts like bringing everything I needed for the day down from my bedroom to avoid having to climb the stairs. There I sat, like a pensioner in a care home with her handbag at her feet.

One morning in June, I woke with my heart pounding and adrenaline coursing through my veins.

Why was I panicking in my sleep? I hadn't had a nightmare. Disoriented, I looked at the clock. 3am. My sleeping pattern was beginning to deteriorate. I had always slept so well; it was perplexing.

I knew people with insomnia shouldn't look at the time as it reinforces their wakefulness, but I was beyond that. I had been diarising my sleep and counting the hours. How could I heal if I could not sleep? I scrolled through my phone to find a calming sleep meditation and put my earphones in, mindful of how lightly Tom slept next to me.

I had a love-hate relationship with meditation. I had heard many times about its benefits, about clearing negative emotions and stress, releasing anxiety about the future and depression about the past, and how it can heal the body. But I found it impossible to clear my mind; even just being alone with my thoughts felt jarring and uncomfortable. My mind was a feedback loop of churning questions or the trivialities of life: whether the kids were safe at school, if my parents and in-laws were safe at home, the washing and cleaning that wasn't being done, what was for tea and the, by now, frequent replays of my Covid drama over and over.

Who had given it to me? Which person in the row was it? Should I approach them about it? Did I even get ill at the school concert? Maybe it was a delivery man at work, or the man behind me in the supermarket. Why can no doctors help me – it's their job to help me…

On, and on. I couldn't turn off the chatter, the endless monologues, the white noise. I was waging war in my head and could not quiet my mind.

As instructed by the honeyed voice, I tried to observe my thoughts and not react to them, to distance myself and acknowledge them. To be aware of awareness.

"Connect to gratitude," said the voice.

I felt anger building inside me.

I am not grateful for this shit! This is not living, this is hell! I have a chronic illness in a global pandemic, no one can help me, there is no cure. How dare she tell me to connect to gratitude! This is a complete fucking waste of time.

I threw my headphones across the bed.

I was averaging three to five hours of sleep a night, yet didn't feel at all tired. In fact, I was completely wired. I wondered why that was. I had no understanding of my condition and there was apparently no one I could reach out to who did. Through a chink in the curtains, I could just make out the shimmer of the moon. Deep within the cluster of sturdy pines that lined the park, an owl hooted. He was often with me at night – the wakeful owl – screeching his warning cry behind a veil of darkness.

As the streetlamps flicked on one by one, I observed the dawn hours tick by, waiting until I could call the surgery again. Wide awake, I grabbed my laptop and in desperation began to research my symptoms on the internet. I stumbled across a Covid support group on Facebook. Wow, so there were others still struggling, too. And not just a few – the group had 10,000 members already. I began to scroll through the posts: people wrote of relapses, lung burn, insomnia, palpitations… it was like reading my own medical history. I learnt that the relapses I was having now had a name: Long Covid. There were no answers, but I was amazed and relieved – I wasn't alone.

At 8am I called the surgery. The familiar hold music clicked in, then the automated response.

"You are number 15 in the queue and your call is important to us."

Forty five minutes later, the receptionist picked up.

"Hello" I said, "I would like a call back from my own doctor, Dr Hampton please." What I actually wanted was a face-to-face appointment, but I knew this was off the table, despite my having tested negative for Covid.

"I'm afraid Dr Hampton isn't available until a week next Tuesday; could I ask Dr. White to call you? He can do between 12 and 5pm."

I sighed. "Sure." Exasperated, I hung up.

This wasn't the way it was supposed to work. I should see my doctor in person, have a physical exam, give a description of the problem, get a diagnosis and a prescription. Then I would take medication and I would get well. That's what happens when you are ill, it's been that way for decades. Doctors do not say they don't know.

The pandemic restrictions had put a stop to even the first part of the process. There was no validation, no information, no cure. Medicine, as I knew it, was failing me. I felt betrayed and helpless.

"The problem with that surgery is that they're chronically understaffed," I said to Tom later in the kitchen. "I get it, it's a pandemic but people like me have to use what little energy we have trying to be heard and I've not spoken to the same doctor twice. It's exhausting. I'm so sick of repeating my story. It's always the same questions: 'Have you had a Covid test?' No, there were none available; 'Do you want to tell me your symptoms… if you have a fever you need to self-isolate again'. There's no continuity of care."

"I know, love," Tom replied. He was adjusting his bike pedals, getting ready to go out. "I don't know how they think they can diagnose people over the phone without looking at them." He stopped what he was doing and looked up, clearly worried. "Do you think you should ask for another blood test?"

I left the question hanging. It was clear I wasn't getting the help I needed but I couldn't blame the doctors for that: they simply did not have the answers. Could alternative therapies work for me? I was unconvinced. I had tried homeopathy in the past: the cost was prohibitive but more than that, I'd found the tinctures, lotions and potions troubling. Drinking a universal elixir felt like a weird alchemy and didn't fit with my world view. I'd felt an uneasy distrust of the person prescribing it and didn't understand his unfamiliar credentials. Was he a fraud? Had he laughed at me and rubbed his hands together after I left his treatment room? I mulled it over. Inertia was not an option; I had to do something.

"Some of the group on Facebook have had success with acupuncture. Maybe I should try that?"

"I don't know" said Tom. "Maybe?"

"I don't know why I'm asking Teflon man anyway," I smirked. "You've never had a day sick in your life; you kiss the person the night before they get Covid symptoms and all germs bounce off you. It's really irritating, you don't even get hangovers. Do you remember when our friends came to stay and brought the flu from the plane, and I was in bed all Christmas day and you were fine? You'll be the last person left on the planet after they drop the bomb."

"Yep, iron man that's me," he replied, pretending to flex his muscles.

Lily came running down the stairs just as he headed out the door.

"Why does Dad wear those funny clothes? He looks like a sea lion."

"There are probably quite a few sea lions out on their bikes today," I smiled, "it's a nice day for a ride."

"Mum, you know the end of year show is coming up… can you come?" she said, practising her leaps and turns on the slippery lino. My heart sank. "You know it's The Lion King and I'm Scar. We can't do proper costumes or anything but we've made masks and they're putting a stage up in the playground. Please will you come?" she begged.

"I've got to see how I am by then, my love. Of course I will if I'm well enough."

After three long months of home schooling, year six children had returned to school along with year ones and reception classes. The question of the show was one I had been dreading.

We were easing out of lockdown but my world had diminished. I had stopped driving – my palpitations made it too dangerous to risk and I had lost my nerve anyway. Going to the show would require me to walk about 200 yards with Tom across the playground. I didn't know if I could manage it. Nor could I bear the thought of being pushed in a wheelchair in front of all the parents. I knew that if I crashed badly again a week before, going anywhere would be impossible. And yet, not going was also not an option. I was also deeply concerned about the risk of reinfection. If I was this ill already then surely catching it again would be easier? Unless I had antibodies, but how long did they last? These thoughts swirled around my synapses most of my waking hours leaving me paranoid and suspicious of everyone. I was on high alert, constantly scanning for threats.

I managed to get an afternoon appointment for my acupuncture treatment. As I lay supine on the massage table in Lisa's warm, cosy practice room we chatted through my symptoms and she took notes.

"I read your email," she said. "I'm sorry to hear all about your symptoms."

"No one seems to know how to cure this," I said. "Do you have any other clients with it?"

"No, but the British Acupuncture Council contacted the Government at the start of the pandemic and suggested we could help support the NHS. Unfortunately they never received a reply, but I do believe acupuncture can help."

"I've heard it's being used in China for people with Long Covid."

"Yes, I've just been reading they've had success with people who've lost their sense of taste and smell. Acupuncture works to help calm the nervous system; it's a holistic practice so it treats the whole body. It turns on neurons that inhibit pain and block pain perception in the brain and it slows down the body's production of stress hormones."

She went on to explain that energy, or 'Qi', moves throughout the body via pathways called meridians. Stress can cause a stagnation of this energy, and when this happens, disruptions to the natural flow of energy can cause disease. Acupuncture releases endorphins which keep the energy flowing and puts the brain into patterns where healing can take place.

I was doubtful. I wasn't stressed, so why would that be affecting my energy flow?

"I'm going to insert needles close to a nerve," she then said. "This causes the nervous system to produce painkilling chemicals and encourages the body's natural ability to heal itself. I'm going to start by feeling your pulse: in Chinese medicine, that's your Qi flowing through the body. Then I'll ask you to take a few deep breaths, okay?"

"Yes." I stared at the patchy ceiling and felt no pain as the needle went in. I tried to stay calm and focus on the music playing in the background, but the exertion of climbing on the high bed had caused my heart to bang in my chest. I willed it to stabilise.

"Okay," she said gently, "I'm just going to pop one between your eyes; this is the Yintang. It has a powerful action of calming the mind and it helps with insomnia and anxiety." She reached for a heated lamp and placed it over my tummy. "This will help keep the torso warm which will improve your circulation and flush any unwanted toxins away."

I heard the door click shut as she left me to my thoughts.

I had no idea of time as I lay prone on the table. Twenty minutes? Ten, thirty? I tried to meditate but again I was thwarted by my distracted, troubled mind and the intense pounding of my heart. Lisa came back in and proceeded to remove the needles.

"I'm going to check your Qi again now. Good," she nodded, feeling my pulse again, "much more grounded; that is what we are looking for."

My heart had been racing during the session, but as I eased off the table, I noticed it had calmed. I felt my blood pressure had lowered too.

"I feel so much better," I said. And I really did.

"Good," she replied. "Your body will begin to release toxins that need to be flushed out so make sure you drink plenty of water over the next few hours. I think we should start you off with six sessions and see how we go with that. Are you taking any supplements?"

"No. I did take some vitamin C a few months back, but nothing since then."

"Okay, I would recommend vitamin C and D, plus vitamin B complex. I would also suggest Stabilium. It's a really incredible supplement from a very deep swimming fish. It was used in Roman times, to prepare the soldiers for battle. It's good for sleep patterns, energy, memory, and mood. Bone broth is also really good, lots of green leafy vegetables to support your nervous system, and spirulina: it's an algae and a great antioxidant."

I had never heard of spirulina but I thanked her as I headed out. Did they sell it in Tesco's? Unlikely. My recent faddy purchases of various tinctures and unusual foods had been met with disdain and scorn within the family. I decided not to mention the Molva Dypterygia fish supplement the Romans used; somehow, I thought Tom's response might overshadow the gains made that day.

Back home I spent the afternoon sat by the window, watching enviously as joggers and dog walkers approached the park gates to enjoy their daily exercise. It was agonising to watch. Just three months ago I'd been a healthy, able-bodied person. Going for a walk was beyond my reach now. Although the acupuncture had revived me, the effects were temporary. I remained limited to very small activities around the house – hoovering and changing the beds sent my heart rate spiralling and were impossible. My goals had become minimal: I was now on a mission to conserve energy to prevent further relapses.

Staring out of the window, my mind took me to a recurring daydream where I was shut inside a circular room with many doors. On my knees in the dark, I tried to see a way out. One of the doors had a chink of light. In desperation, I got up and staggered toward it, my fingertips reaching out, but it slammed shut and was padlocked from the outside. I slumped back to my knees.

That evening, we watched Boris Johnson announce that we were "past the peak of this disease". *Not for me*, I thought. I had not flattened the curve, I was ominously anticipating yet another spike. I still had no clear idea of what was wrong with me; numerous blood tests had been inconclusive. Our holiday in Cornwall was approaching, and I was filled with conflicting emotions of anxiety and excitement. I desperately wanted to stay well for the trip, we'd not had a family break for so long and the kids were so excited. I wanted to sleep well, eat nutritious food, get outside in my favourite woodland and eliminate Covid from my world forever, starting with the next seven sacred days of freedom. But, I felt I was getting weaker. Would I be able to smell the salty air from the garden? Would I be well enough to walk on the beach?

Anxious as I was, even I did not envisage what Cornwall had in store for me.

Chapter 4

Salt Water

The sun was high in the sky as we sped along lush, high green hedges. Wild oxeye daisies, cow parsley and cowslips waved gently in the breeze. Offshore, darker clouds were gathering; I knew inclement weather was due for the week, but I didn't care: we were free. The packed car heaved under the weight of our belongings as we slowed down for occasional horses and their riders, carefully negotiating the single-track lane into the dense forest.

As we turned a corner and made our way down the steep-sided stream valley, we snatched glimpses of a little slate cottage amidst the ancient woodland of douglas fir and spruce. Our destination.

We turned into the driveway and pulled up in front of the porch, the children dashing out of the car to explore the garden. Stepping out carefully, I inhaled the scent of evergreen pines and was overcome with yearning. How I wished I could walk behind the cottage, through the picket fence into the familiar woodland glade! I had learnt that a walk in the woods was therapeutic, proven to reduce anxiety. But the edge of those beckoning trees was like a foreign land to me now and I had no passport to travel; I could only manage a few steps from the car into the house. *Next year I will do it*, I vowed. I had read that pine tea could be used to help ease respiratory congestion, support healthy digestion and calm the nervous system, so I resolved to make myself some with the needles.

I could already hear the kids scrambling excitedly up the bank, past the bracken and bramble to the tree swing as Tom brought in the bags. It was small but perfect: just far enough away from civilisation, a true escape from the last few wretched months. We could pretend all was well here.

I would be 44 tomorrow. I had Long Covid, I was unable to walk far but I was alive, and I treasured every moment I had with my family. I thought about the many times Tom and I had prioritised the wrong things in our lives. Doing DIY, jobs, filing, endless repetitive tidying, commuting, and working late, hastily snatched meals before the next drop-off, the mundane but stressful rituals of family life. Had I been happy living like that? Truly content? Why had I wasted my time living upside down, chasing endless horizons, goals that were just out of reach, something I would achieve tomorrow or the next day or next year if I only just had enough money or time? Why did I put off what I should have been doing in the now?

I desperately wanted to run in the fields and dance with my kids, to see the sunrise, build bonfires, swim in the ocean. When all these things are taken from you, it sharpens the focus. *When I am well*, I thought, *I will do them all. I will not wait, I'll live every day in the present*.

The next morning I was pleased and surprised to find that I had slept reasonably well. As the rest of the family slept, I shuffled down to the kitchen to make a ginger tea. The sky was bright, so I headed to the patio and sat down on one of the two wrought-iron chairs. Shivering in the chilly morning air, I hugged my cardigan around me and sipped my tea.

I absentmindedly inspected the tufty grass and weeds surrounding the rockery nearby and kicked at some loose pebbles. A shady patch of violets caught my eye; it seemed to be moving. Looking closer, I realised it was teeming with life. More silver-washed fritillary caterpillars than I had ever seen were moving rhythmically just yards from my feet, hundreds of them. Their black-brown bodies slowly shifted in an undulating, harmonious wave, two pale lines marking their long, reddish-brown spiky spines.

I continued to study them as they made their slow migration across the path, up the four-metre south-facing wall to construct their cocoons in its lofty heights. Several of their number were already safely enshrined in the wall, commencing their metamorphosis. A caravan of courageous little nomads, climbing that sheer edge to make their transformation into a new expression of life. So patient and hardy. Nature governed that they were unable to grow in their current form; unquestioningly they shed the past to make way for a better version of themselves. They were a wonder.

The birthday celebrations were enjoyable, if muted. The girls had baked a Victoria sponge cake and I allowed myself half a glass of fizz to acknowledge the day. But by mid-afternoon the sky was an ashen grey and storm clouds were gathering from the west. The temperature dropped and the wind chimes on the outside wall began to strike a doleful, broken chord. Drops were beginning to fall and soon rain was lashing the windows and running in rivulets down the stone walls.

I felt there was a definite link between the foods I was eating and my symptoms, and had noticed my appetite was becoming suppressed. I had asked for a Nutribullet for my birthday on the recommendation of one of the group, and as I unwrapped the package, I hoped the fresh fruit juices that I would prepare would reduce the dull pains that had returned in my legs. I was keen to regain the weight I'd lost with extra calories outside of the anti-inflammatory meals I was trying. My latest diet was low histamine; I would miss dairy, but I felt empowered to try something new.

We passed the time with puzzles and card games the owners had left behind as mist and drizzle enveloped the house. We planned the next few days' events: a bike ride for the kids and we would still go to the beach, although I doubted I'd be able to get onto the sand – I had become very weak.

The Wi-Fi was intermittent in the house so by the time we drove up out of the valley towards the coast the next day, our phones were pinging with updates.

A second wave of Coronavirus is starting across mainland Europe ... U.S. death toll tops 170,000 ... Rishi Sunak launches Eat Out to Help Out, WHO encourages all nations to work together on Covid vaccine...

I hurriedly switched off the phones. Just the word Covid could make my stomach lurch and I wanted to be free of that today. We passed windswept walkers braving the leaden skies as gulls swooped above us, cawing their raucous cries, battered and frequently knocked off course by the irrepressible force of nature. The heather and gorse of the headland gave way to mist-shrouded fishing villages and harbours dotted with clusters of hardy holiday makers in waterproofs and wellies heading doggedly to join others on the pier clutching crabbing lines and buckets.

We navigated the final bend of the coast road and dropped down towards the sheltered estuary. The Toyota hummed and ticked over as we queued along the flat, single road to the beach, the windscreen wipers counting time. Drumming the dashboard impatiently, I stared at the blurry red brake lights of the vehicle in front. I hadn't come on holiday to sit in the car, but it seemed the whole world was here with us in this tiny inlet. Families were three abreast on the thin pavement strip that bordered the shoreline and others were jostling past them trying to avoid the cars in the queue. There was no two-metre rule here, no social distancing; everyone seemed to have forgotten the preventative protocols.

I craned my head to view our old holiday rental as we inched past, remembering the halcyon days of past summers there with the family, the grandparents, cousins, dogs. We were carefree then, no knowledge of family bubbles, masks, or distancing. No sanctions or constraints, no notion of the value of our liberty – we were kings and queens of our own rule. Our castle had been a flat fronted Victorian terrace with a patio garden out the back. The joy of cramming all ten of us in the few bedrooms plus three dogs in the laundry was unimaginable to me now. We were right on the estuary, partitioned from pavement walkers by a waist-high, dry-stone wall. The teenagers would pull on their wetsuits and race out the front door, dogs yapping excitedly at their heels, paddles clasped tightly in their hands. They would cross the road and head down the slipway to the shallows, carefully picking their way over the treacherous rocks and algae, squealing as they went, to launch their boards on the outgoing tide. The adults would sip steamy coffees and watch the boats bobbing on the creek from the comfort of their enclosed suntrap out front, while the world sauntered slowly past.

We had come to an abrupt halt; it was evident that the car park was full. Vehicles were turning around. We followed suit and trailed back 300 yards to the nearest space on the road. There was nowhere else to stop and nowhere to wait. Walking that far would be impossible for me: there were no seats, and I didn't have a wheelchair. The sand was a wheelchair's nemesis anyway, I knew that already from spending time with Dad. I was trapped. There was no option but to agree that I would stay in the car, they would get a takeaway drink and then go for a walk on the beach without me. They said goodbye and one by one the doors slammed shut, their figures disappearing into the murky distance.

As I focused on the sea beyond the windshield, my tears, the ocean, and the rain blurred and fused before my eyes. Blues and greys, salt water. My world was closing in. I was a captive in my own body, imprisoned where I no longer felt safe. The cruelty of this disease knew no bounds. Here I was alone, desperate for a way out. Rubbing my eyes, I sunk down low in the seat, retreating below the dashboard to hide my blotchy face from view. I stayed like that sobbing for a long time.

And then it happened. The all-too-familiar pattern of dread, the rush of inflammation to my legs: I was crashing again. Alone in the car, the spectre of Covid loomed.

No, no, no, not now, I'm already too weak, my body can't take it again. Please.

I grabbed my bag at my feet, clawing for water, paracetamol, something, anything to stem the flow. Every other time Tom had been there with me to hold my hand, to help soothe me through it, but he was gone. This time I would have to brave it on my own.

My head jolted back, immobile, concreted to the headrest and my jaw clamped shut, skin stretched tight around my mouth. My heart was pulsating in my back. Knowing all too well what would come next, I made fists, nails cutting into the skin on my palms as adrenaline surged through my body. My torso clenched momentarily before turning involuntarily rigid. An excruciating, deadening weight of burning inflammation pressed on every fibre of my body, forcing me down flat as I tried to equalise, to come up for air, while the intense pressure held me under. Then nausea and convulsing involuntarily in waves – an anamnesis of past ills, free radicals coursing through my body – limbs shaking. I knew that weight loss would follow as every ounce of latent energy was cleaved from me.

I felt strangely calm, unable to speak or call for help. There I lay, helpless, wounded, until the fever peaked and the shaking subsided. My brain was misfiring, but I understood enough to realise our holiday was over. I was gravely ill.

Chapter 5

A Dowser Calls

It was September and I was sat in my favourite chair by the bedroom window, blanket on my knee. Staring at the dog walkers in the park, I summoned the energy to answer my phone. It was my childhood friend, Gemma.

"How are you?" she asked.

Where to begin.

"I'm not right, Gem. I feel like I'm getting worse and I've no idea what's wrong with me. I'm losing so much weight. I've got diarrhoea, I can barely stand. Everything hurts. I have insomnia, I dread the nights …" I forced myself to stop my tale of woe. I didn't mention the lump. If I mentioned it, I knew it would become real.

"What do the doctors say?"

"The doctors can't help. They say it's just 'multiple Long Covid symptoms', but how is that a diagnosis let alone a prognosis? There's also this warped idea that if you're not dead then you're fine, but we're supposed to be thriving, right? I'm a long way from thriving. Our holiday was terrible. I was so poorly, Tom had to carry me down the stairs and we had to go home after three days. I don't feel safe in my own body. And, I'm scared."

It was true; I had become afraid of being myself.

"I'm so sorry to hear this," Gemma replied. "I've been thinking about you so much. I thought as I hadn't heard that perhaps you still weren't right. Have you tried any alternative therapies?"

"I've been having acupuncture since my first relapse in June. I always feel better afterwards but it doesn't last long."

"You poor thing. I wish I could help."

"Thanks, love. I know," I whispered.

"Have you heard about the Medical Medium in America?"

"No, who is that? Like a psychic?"

"Yes, Anthony William. He's a healer, he's been featured on that website Goop and works with lots of stars. He diagnosed his grandmother with lung cancer when he was a boy. He's written books on it."

"I need a miracle right now, but he must cost a fortune and he's in America, right?"

"Yeah."

"Sorry Gem, I'm so tired I need to go now."

Days passed and I grew steadily weaker. My symptoms could change from hour to hour but I was largely bedridden. My hair began to fall out in clumps and I had difficulty bathing myself. My tachycardia peaked with any low level exertion and I had numbness in my fingers. I couldn't regulate my body temperature; it was as though my internal thermostat was broken. Not knowing what was wrong with me was extremely disconcerting.

Long Covid was barely in the news, but there were now 40,000 people on the Facebook group. No one was helping us and it felt like we were screaming into the void. To me, Long Covid was a shadowy, formless disease with no clinical history and no known prognosis. Just the name sounded ominous. I remembered my friend who had been diagnosed with a tumour in her neck. Instead of calling it cancer, she had named it Doris. In this way she had disarmed it and removed its psychological sting.

A revolving door of doctors were doing their best to give me a diagnosis: blood tests had been sent for Lymes Disease, Cocksakie, Babesia, Bartonella, EBV and even for enteric organisms. All had returned normal. But I was feeling far from normal. It had become extremely difficult to control my emotions. I was chronically depressed and a deep sense of sadness often ended in uncontrollable sobbing. I felt terribly afraid with an awful sense of foreboding, as if fear had been downloaded into my subconscious programming. I would find myself sitting for long periods just thinking about what was happening to me, reliving the initial fever and lung damage and those days in the box room. Isolated in the house and away from social contact, my phone was my only lifeline.

In desperation one night, we called my parents. We had run out of ideas and needed support from the wider family. I felt the weight of the burden that Tom was carrying: it was too much for one person, along with everything else he had to deal with.

"Julie, it's Tom. Can we talk?"

"How is she?" Mum broke in.

"I'm afraid this is going to be very hard to hear. She's in a terrible state. I don't know how to help her and she's getting worse. She can't get out of bed, I can't stop her crying. She's in chronic pain, says she has heart problems. She's worried she's dying."

Mum inhaled sharply.

"I feel like we've exhausted all avenues," he continued. "The doctors don't know what else to do. I'm so worried. I feel like I've failed her." His voice broke.

"You have not failed, Tom, you have been incredible; no one could have done more. This is beyond all of us. We're not medically trained. Can you put her on?"

"I can but you remember how exhausted she gets."

"I know."

Tom handed me the phone.

"Nic, it's Mum. Don't speak, just listen. I've been speaking to my friend Judy. She knows someone, I don't really understand it but he's like a healer, it's alternative. It's called dowsing. I don't know what that is, but do you want to try it? He doesn't charge anything."

"Yes Mum I do," was all I could manage as my head fell back on the pillow. I passed the phone back.

"I've spoken to him and he's going to call you tonight," she said to Tom.

"Ok, thank you Julie. Speak soon."

Tom's eyes were filled with tears. We hugged and cried together, holding each other through our pain.

"I wish I knew how to help you."

"You are helping me," I said, "but we have to get real. If I've got breast cancer as well as Long Covid, I'm afraid it's goodnight Irene. I can't fight a war on two fronts."

"Don't say that!" he sobbed, "I can't do any of this without you." The phone rang. Tom swallowed hard and wiped his eyes. "I think this is him."

"Hello?"

"Hi there, Tom is it?"

"That's right."

"Yes hello, it's about Nicola isn't it? I've spoken to her mum briefly. I was obviously very saddened to hear of her health problems. Rest assured I will do everything I can to try and help, though it's obviously impossible to give any guarantees. On the bright side, it usually works! My wife calls me a naturopath when she tells people about me, but I'm not, I'm a dowser."

"Sure, ok," said Tom. He had no idea what a dowser was.

"I just need to speak to her very briefly."

"Okay, but I'm afraid she's very poorly. Speaking is hard for her, she gets exhausted and can't concentrate for long."

"I had ME myself in the 80s, I understand."

Tom passed me the phone.

"Hello? It's John."

"Hi John."

"I know you're very poorly, I've been in your position myself. I was given antibiotics by a locum doctor in the 80s, I took them and they destroyed my microbiome. I was bedridden and off work for nine months. Allopathic medicine couldn't help me; I had to look elsewhere."

On some level the word microbiome registered with me, but I couldn't recall its significance.

"I'll be quick," he went on. "I need to ask you a few questions. So I have your full name? Address here?"

"Yes, that's right."

"Ok, so tell me a little about what you like to do. Hobbies, that sort of thing."

The banality of the question threw me – I was expecting a more clinical line of enquiry. "Um, well when I was well I walked a lot, I like dancing ballet…" I trailed off, searching for memories of my lost former life.

"And where do you go as a family on holiday?"

As I summoned all my strength to reply, I wondered how this was helping. Why on earth did he need to know about my holidays? And where I lived? How would that cure me?

"We normally go to Cornwall. I love the sea."

"Ah yes, I don't get the chance to go down there much these days but St. Ives was always our spot. Great, thanks, okay you can pass me back to Tom now."

Exhausted, I rubbed my forehead. Bizarre, truly bizarre. *What is he going to do with that information?* I wondered. My life had taken a very surreal turn.

Tom put the phone down. "He says he has all the information he needs and will call back in a couple of hours." He looked perplexed. "How can he know how to help you from that? Without even seeing you? He didn't even ask about your symptoms. In fact, he asked not to know."

"He knew I had Covid, but that's all. I just don't understand it. What is a dowser? Is that like dowsing for water? It's rods isn't it, and walking over the ground? What does that have to do with healing?"

"I'm praying it's not cancer," said Tom, an anguished look on his face.

I felt so confused. The old me would be scouring the internet and ordering books, finding out everything possible about dowsing for health. But I was weak and disoriented; reading anything was out of the question. I felt as though I was half waking, half dreaming, or playing the lead part in a harrowing, far-fetched film. I lay back on the pillow.

Tom brought dinner up on a tray. I forced a little down, but it stuck in my throat and my stomach burned. My clothes were starting to hang off me and I could feel my ribs jutting out from under my t-shirt. I no longer had the strength to walk down the stairs.

When the phone rang again, we held hands. My heart thumped as I braced for the breast cancer diagnosis.

"Hi John it's Tom, you're on speaker phone, please go ahead."

"I believe that Nicola has a fungal infection in her gut which is compromising her immune system."

My eyes widened. Inexplicably, I felt he was right.

"I'm getting that she had Covid in March, but the current viral presence of COV2 in her body is now very low. It's clear she's at an extremely low ebb. I use key markers for her functions, these are the percentage results. You're really looking for at least 80% plus in each of these areas; please bear in mind 0% does not mean you are dead and 100% does not mean you're an Olympic athlete! These are simply status progress indicators of my own making.

"I'm afraid some of these are extremely low values. Now, where are my notes… here we are. Overall vitality 0%, immune system function 30%, immune system activity 40%, (a value of 50% is normal 'tick over', at 60% it is dealing with something, at 40% a pathogen is present, but it isn't being dealt with effectively), endocrine function 50%, neural network function 40%, muscle function 10%, digestive group function 10%, nervous system function 10%."

Tom scribbled notes frantically as I tried to process what John was saying.

"In total I dowse for 250 vitamins and minerals in the body," he went on. "The good news is that of all the values and indicators I dowse, 159 of yours give no cause for concern. It's obvious that up to a certain point in time you have looked after yourself pretty well.

"It's clear from my results that this is not simply a case of problems post Covid-19, or rather SARS-COV2, which is the actual virus. My results suggest that there were underlying gut issues before Covid came along, so in a sense you're having to deal with an overlay of multiple problems. It's only in the last twenty years that science has realised the true importance of gut health and its critical role in the prevention of disease. We're all asymptomatic carriers of trillions of bacteria and hundreds of trillions of viruses. Most organisms are not fatal to us. Historically, bacteria, viruses and fungi have been regarded as a sort of enemy to be eliminated. We had been getting things badly wrong."

I thought back to my mouth ulcers and occasional mild reflux and constipation, all symptoms of poor digestion that I accepted as normal for me and not worth bothering any doctor with. How could John possibly know about that?

"Science is now fully aware that in most cases, just the opposite is true," he continued. "Most of the genetic material in our body is bacterial or viral in nature and responsible for producing key vitamins, hormones and controlling our mood. The connection between gut and brain, notably via the vagus nerve, is critical. It's interesting to note that in terms of communication, the gut sends about ten messages to the brain for every one sent by the brain to the gut. Guess what, 70% of your immune system resides in the gut and is fuelled by the gut!

"To say the gut is important is an understatement. Mostly, you are not feeding *you* but your gut microbiome. The microbiome and virome are terms you will come to see much more of in the future but sadly, for the moment, allopathic medicine hasn't caught up with mainstream science (and typically takes twenty years or more to do so). However, apologies I am veering off topic..."

He paused. I waited impatiently for him to continue.

"This period has, I suspect, been preceded by some relatively mild digestive issues and had Covid not arrived they would perhaps have passed, or could have been fixed fairly quickly. Covid has compounded this and added to it, but while it has depleted many of the nutrients involved in the body's first line of defence, it has not devastated, or even barely touched, many of those known to be involved in the more serious defences. For example, your levels of vitamin C, D, zinc and so on are perfectly normal.

"Er so, the obvious plan of attack would be to improve gut health and hence the health of your immune system. But, given the shortage of nutrients to do so and the dubious ability of the gut to process them well, we're in a bit of a chicken and egg situation. What I've decided to do is to ignore the loss of what we might call more specialised nutrients and see if we can build up some of the more basic ones that are seriously depleted – basic in the sense that they are typical causes of any major fatigue, loss of drive and an inability to concentrate. The prime reason for this is that you cannot be expected to supplement all the things that have been depleted, there are far too many and in any event you need most of these 'basic' nutrients to allow the body to properly process others."

He paused.

"Are you still with me?"

"Yes,' replied Tom. By now, he had stopped writing anything down.

"I must be clear that this is something of a 'suck it and see' situation because the body's operation is so complex. For example, one might be short of twenty things, but only need ten of them, the other ten being restored automatically. Conversely, you might have twenty nutrients that look perfect and ten that are depleted. But when you supplement the ten, many of the twenty suddenly start to drop. The logic is simple, the twenty were only 'perfect' because the body had not been using them due to the missing ten! We simply must make a start and see what your body does with its newfound nutrients.

"I'll prepare an email to you tonight to follow up with my recommendations and suggested supplement regime. One more thing: you don't have to understand what I do, you just need to follow my advice. I realise this is an unusual way of treating you and I am asking a lot for you to trust me on this. All the best now and I'll be in touch."

Stunned, we hung up the phone.

Chapter 6

The Numbers

I'm hallucinating a chaotic hypnopompic dream sequence. Images of people I don't recognise flash through my head in a staccato slideshow. My body is being shocked with electricity and I'm downloading information in the pictures at an incredible speed. As conscious and subconscious collide I jolt back into my body, ripped away from sleep again.

It was 3am. Panting, heart pounding, tears came. I was failing fast and knew I needed to formulate a plan while I could still function. I'd read about a man who recovered from chronic fatigue after moving in with his parents on an isolated Scottish island many miles from his home. His tale inspired me. Nudging Tom awake, I explained my drastic proposal. I knew he would trust my judgement implicitly, but my emotional intelligence had left me. I didn't even ask him if he'd be okay, if he could look after work, the girls, the house and the dog on his own, if he could manage. I could only think about my own failing body. I was becoming deeply introspective.

We waited for as long as we could before making the call. My parents gathered round the screen in their pyjamas, their faces lined and ashen with concern. I could barely move or respond but it was agreed that I would leave that day.

It was a terrible moment. The thought of leaving my children went against every fibre of my being as a mother. The girls had always come first, always; how could I willingly leave them? The mental torture of separation was worse than any physical pain. I was their mum: they needed me and I desperately needed them, but the reality was I had no energy to have them anywhere near me. How long would we be separated for? A future without them in my life was unthinkable. I was inconsolable.

One after the other, they shuffled in to say goodbye. I desperately wanted to be strong for them, as I was supposed to, as I would have been when I was well, but I couldn't hold back the tears. I hated them seeing me like that. Ella held my hand; Lily sobbed as she gave me a hug and a kiss goodbye – and then they were gone. Deep in my mind, in the room where dark night poured in, another door slammed shut.

Lying on the back seat of the car, I watched the macabre silhouettes of trees flash by. Fleeting glimpses of an autumn azure sky came and went, leaves making their spiralling descent, twisting and tumbling, caught in the gusts, wrestling against the ultimate force of the earth.

I tried to process what was happening to me. I had always pictured my life in markers, of rites of scripted passage, always moving forwards – a natural trajectory of birth, teenage, marriage, work, parenting, retirement, death. But now I seemed to have stopped travelling – I was stuck somewhere, sent outside of time and space. Either the clock had stopped ticking, or it had accelerated. In this limbo, every wretched hour was lifeless and still while the world outside continued to turn. Or, maybe

I was living life upside down, returning to my childhood, living life as a helpless baby. Or was I in the future somehow: had I skipped a generation, joined my parents and was living out my old age prematurely? Were these my last days?

As the car drew up, I heard the familiar crunch of the gravel driveway. Mum was standing in her apron and slippers, ready to help me up the stone steps to the flat. The exertion of getting out of the car caused my heart to pound heavily in my chest. Shooting pains travelled down my legs and along my arms; I felt heady and nauseous. I hesitated. I couldn't process my goodbye to Tom, the enormity of it. We both underplayed it and few words were spoken. I held him, told him briefly I would text him, and then he was gone.

I looked up at the imposing Edwardian building, home to eight flats. My parents had the sweeping entrance with grand, black double doors. Elderly neighbours with shared entrances were shielding in adjoining flats above and next door. A curtain twitched from an upper window and fell back as I glanced up. I pulled myself up the five steps, through the small hall and into the spare room.

This room was my new home.

The French doors to the balcony framed the bright blue September sky and patchwork fields beyond the garden. Vibrant, lime-green wisteria twisted against the black iron balustrade that ran along the width of the house. A robin perched on a terracotta planter outside as I eased myself onto the low bed. I remembered that hospital patients with a view of nature recovered more quickly. Waiting for my heart to calm a little from the exertion, I allowed myself to feel thankful for this calming setting.

Mum had put two framed pictures of the children by my bed. I took in their gappy smiles, the fresh flowers on the mantle. This was a world of freshly laundered sheets, doilies and Union Jack bunting. Mum busied herself unpacking my bag and bringing towels and water. We had spoken many times about old age, Mum and I. I'd always imagined looking after her, not the reverse, not this. She'd always joked that when she was doubly incontinent I was to 'finish her off', to take her to Dignitas. I understood fully now why people didn't want to continue living cruelly compromised lives.

As the sun streamed in, I heard my parents in the lounge log on and the printer whirr into action. The thin walls did little to mask their conversation.

"We're wasting our time," moaned Dad. "She's in such a terrible state and we've got some pseudoscientist giving her false hope. It's like witchcraft, Julie, and I don't like it. It's dangerous, she should be seeing real doctors."

"Look, she's tried everything," said Mum, "there's nothing else we can do. Judy says she can't explain it, but John's got everything right for her and you know she's had Long Covid too, not as badly obviously, but she says it's working for her. He's been helping her for years. She said he's helped thousands of people recover from various things."

Dad grumbled and loaded up Amazon.

"What is dowsing anyway? There's no evidence for it," he muttered. "Remember last time when we messed with that Ouija board with your mother? That ended in tears."

"That was fifty years ago! And that is absolutely nothing like this."

I thought back to the folkloric tale of their dabbling with Ouija boards as young adults. My maternal grandmother was deeply spiritual and would frequently hold séances around her kitchen table. She looked the part, her platinum hair piled high on her head, shawl over her shoulders, glasses perched on her nose and her nimble hands darting back and forth as she set up the board. She relished contacting her mother long since passed, but my father had been deeply spooked one night when the board foretold of a seemingly improbable event involving the death of an older aunt. It played out exactly as the board had described, even down to the location and timeframe. Dad forbade my mother from ever touching it again.

"Pass me the email and I'll read the list out to you," he said.

"Good God, what are all these things?" said Mum, "I've never heard of most of them."

"Bring my glasses over will you, Julie? Hang on, HANG. ON. Amazon is still loading. How are you spelling Methyl Folate?"

"I told you Malc, M. E. T…"

"What does 1000ug mean?"

"That's the measurement; John says 1000ug is the same as 1mg."

"How do you spell Lycopene? These words are all unfamiliar to me."

"I just told you how you spell it. Good grief this is like pulling teeth," sighed Mum. "I need a cup of tea."

"Any cake, Julie?"

Dad continued his battle with the supplement order. It was long:

After breakfast:

1 Methyl Folate
1 B Complex 100
2 Lutein/lycopene/Carotene
2 Chromium Picolinate
1 Vitamin A
1 teaspoon of D-Ribose powder in water (as label)

After lunch:

1 Gamma E
1 Phos Choline
1 Phos Serine
1 N-Aceytl Cysteine
1 teaspoon of D-Ribose

After evening meal:

1 Gamma E
1 B Complex 100
1 Lutein/lycopene/Carotene
1 Phosphatidyl Choline
1 Phosphatidyl Serine
1 Chromium Picolinate
1 teaspoon D-Ribose

Late evening:

1 L-Methionine

Somehow, Dad managed to place the order. Then he read out the rest of John's email.

"The L-METH-EIO-ER-NINE..." he stumbled with a mouthful of fruit cake.

"It's METHIO-NINE," she corrected. "Why do you add r's to everything?"

"Okay, you know what I mean, stop interrupting. This is what he says; I'm going to read it to you..."

L Methionine is an amino acid and must be taken on an empty stomach; everything else should be taken immediately after food.

Now, I do appreciate this is a lot, but then it is not a small problem. Many of the tablets are tiny, though a few are rather large. The second issue is the fact that Nicola has lost her appetite. I can only say please try to eat; she does not want to take these things on an empty stomach (Methionine excepted). In addition, if what she eats can contain some fats (avocado, sardines, salmon, tuna etc.) that will help a lot with the lunch and evening meal supplements.

Finally, she is clearly in a very stressful situation, but there is nothing worse than stress for degrading immune function so please try to help her relax as much as she can and if possible, get as much fresh air as she can (sit in garden, ideally with bare feet on grass).

It's clear this is not going to be easy, but the problem has to be classed as severe and has gone on for a long time, further compounded by a lack of desire to eat – not a criticism, a consequence of the situation.

Please let me know when you have got all the items and are ready to begin. I need to know when you start and I will keep a track of your numbers once a week, a typical update would be three weeks after.

"Well, I don't get the bit about bare feet on the grass," said Dad. "Sounds a bit Haight Ashbury to me."

"Not a very helpful comment, Malc." Mum poked her head around the door. "Are you sleeping?"

"No, I'm trying not to sleep in the day, it affects the nights," I replied. "Although they're terrible anyway; I dread them."

"I brought you some magazines. They're Saga ones I'm afraid, but some of the articles are quite interesting. You know your father and I are old gits." She chuckled as she put the magazines on the side table.

I managed a weak smile.

"Mum, I need to change my diet to a Candida diet. You know, for the fungal infection. It will need to be quite strict, not like ones I've done before." I inspected my tongue using my compact. "It's really white" I said, sticking my tongue out for Mum to see.

"That will get better," she said kindly. "We'll get the food delivery and make sure we order what you need. John said you need to be drinking three litres of good quality water; he says the stuff we get from the tap is full of hormones and toxins. Mind you, I drink it all the time and it's not been a problem for me. But while you're ill you should have the good stuff." She smiled. "You're going to be ok, you know."

I rubbed my forehead. "Mum, I'm worried I'm going to die." A tear ran down my cheek. "I don't know how much my heart can withstand all of this. It's not functioning properly. I thought it was strong before, but I'm not sure now. I also can't stop crying,"

I sniffed. "You know I'm normally so much stronger than this."

"You are not going to die because I won't let you."

Others had told me I was going to be ok, too. My cousin had come over and spoken to me about his mental health and how he'd recovered. *You'll recover too*, he'd said, but it had made me angry. *It's not the same*, I'd thought, *he can't possibly know. No one has a crystal ball; this is completely different: this is an unknown virus with no cure. None of them know, no one knows. Stop telling me what you think I need to hear.*

I still had to tell Mum about the lump, but couldn't imagine the words leaving my lips. How could I tell her?

I focused on what she was saying.

"John says heart regulation is connected to the gut, so maybe we have to fix your digestion and then your heart will right itself."

"Maybe." I was doubtful.

"I know you're not sure about God, but you know the village church group are all praying for you. They've even set up a Zoom group, and your father and I pray for you every night."

"That's nice Mum, thank you." I felt humbled that people who'd never met me would pray for me. I was glad I had all bases covered.

It was true I was agnostic; my strong church upbringing had pushed religion out of me and I was left feeling vacant and confused. In my heart I felt that the complexity of the world and nature couldn't be a freak accident, but I subscribed to the 'seeing is believing' model. Empiricist. How could God exist and let people suffer like this?

I needed the bathroom. I shuffled along the corridor using

the walls as my crutch. I hated going: the palpitations on exertion and the pain in my legs were barely to be endured, but beyond that I loathed seeing myself in the full-length mirror. My eyes were sunken, my hair grey and lank; bald patches had begun to appear on my scalp. My skin was pinched tight over my cheeks and my shoulders revealed a protruding torso. A fatless skeleton of hung bones. Back in the bedroom, I laboriously propped up the pillows again and scanned my phone. Somewhere locked in the repository of my brain, I knew that the first step to recovery was acceptance. I had to surrender to whatever was happening and stop fighting it. I had to accept that my body was essentially broken and that I couldn't do the things I used to do. There was no room for denial.

I had felt low level anxiety since the start of 2020. I remembered discussions with Tom leading up to March – how incredulous I'd been that he wasn't panicking about the wave of disease washing up on our shores. Why didn't he care, why wasn't he in a state of turmoil? His simple response was that he couldn't get stressed about something he couldn't control. For him, fear and panic were a waste of energy and couldn't affect the outcome. I understood that now, and was beginning to understand how damaging this constant state of fear had been to my body.

I set out on a mission to research chronic fatigue. If that's what I was slipping into, I wanted to explore everything there was to know about it. I had to know all about the appalling reality of what I was facing. We'd done Belkin personality profiles at work a few years back: I was a 'resource investigator', off the scale. This would be kill or cure for me now.

The stats jumped out of my phone and hit me hard.

… a median recovery rate of 5%… CFS, also known as ME is as disabling and has a greater impact on functional status and well-being than other chronic diseases such as cancer… you have to be lucky to recover…

Lucky? How can recovery be a game of roulette? I was appalled. I was desperate to be home by Christmas, but I had no idea how my story ended.

Days passed. The latest catchy slogan beaming out from the television was *hands, face, space*. Locked inside as ill as I was, it barely resonated with me at all. I was fixated on the agonising wait for my supplements.

My symptoms were many and varied. I had small, raised lumps on my skin which I suspected were from the herpes virus, although I had no way of confirming my suspicions. I had numb hands, blurred vision and an extremely unsettling internal body vibration. I had chronic pain in my arms and legs, no appetite, and I was painfully thin. I cried often, but always within the privacy of my bedroom. Washing was energy sapping; Mum would bring me a silver bowl and flannel with a bar of Dove soap and fresh towels every day. Walking the few steps to the bathroom was a struggle.

In my mind, the supplements were the silver bullet that would fix me. I obsessed over their delivery, constantly tracking their progress online. My relief was palpable when finally they arrived and I could start taking my daily vitamins.

The phone was ringing.

"It's John for you," Mum said, bringing the phone to the bed. She put him on speaker phone.

"Nicola, hello. Well you certainly got the supplements organised quickly!"

"My parents have been great."

"Have you got very bad brain fog?"

"Not very bad, but I do find I can't regulate my temperature – I'm either boiling cold or freezing hot." I paused, confused and awkward, but he ignored my malapropism. It was truly strange not to be able to speak coherently.

"Now, it's important to take these supplements together but spaced out through the day, as I indicated. The reason for this is that most metabolic pathways involve numerous nutrients to do their job properly; they all need to be working in harmony to do that.

"Don't expect a quick improvement – and if you do get one, make sure you don't capitalise on it. For some of the nutrients with pretty low values it usually takes a minimum of two weeks for them to come up, typically three, and they need to be kept there for another three before overreacting to any improvement. You've been at ground zero for many months, remember, although I do believe we have caught this in time."

I let these last words wash over me. Inwardly I allowed myself a modicum of relief; a tiny seed of hope had been planted.

"The best way I can describe it," he continued, "is with the analogy of a battery. A 12-volt battery may well read 12 volts on a meter but if it isn't in good shape and hasn't been charged properly, then as soon as you put a load on it, the voltage will collapse and you will have to start charging it again. It has the potential but no capacity to deliver what is needed!"

The analogy was lost on me. I struggled to understand what he was saying; it was like my cerebral cortex could not process simple concepts anymore.

"Lastly, water," he went on. "The numbers relating to that are not as good as they should be. A working brain is about 80 percent water and all neurological processing is highly dependent on that. You will often hear that the brain is 50 percent fat – it is, fats are critical, hence Phos Choline and Phos Serine. But that's the situation when a brain is out of the body and not in operation. The brain is very prone to dehydration, hence the need for plenty of water. You should be drinking around 2.5 litres a day to aid your recovery."

I thought back with regret about how little water I used to drink: just caffeine-laced tea every few hours, followed by wine at the weekends. I must have been in a constant state of dehydration.

"I do worry about my brain fog," I said. "I used to be reasonably sharp, but now I can't think straight at all. I keep making odd mistakes. And I'm alarmed about my hair – it's falling out in clumps."

"Don't worry about that," he said. "The Phos Serine and Phos Choline will help with the normal functioning of the neuronal cell membranes and should help improve memory. L Methionine will also help with brain function, along with your hair loss. It's clear your body took quite a knock from Covid – it's depleted your vitamin levels which were probably low to begin with. I'm sure the minerals used in the normal functioning of the brain were no exception."

"I will check your numbers again in a few weeks."

I sank back in the bed and felt a glimmer of hope. Was I beginning to trust this man, a man I had never met, with my recovery, with my life?

Chapter 7

Second Wave

Mum came in with my mid-morning snack: mackerel, avocado and hummus on rye crackers. Seeing my glum expression, she sighed.

"You've been so quiet Nic, these past few days. Keep your chin up; I know this is so hard for you away from your family, but this absolutely will not last forever."

"I know. I feel like this disease is sapping my personality. I just feel so withdrawn." I felt a mute, intense sorrow, as if the life blood had drained from me.

"Maybe it's a way of your body conserving energy," said Mum. "But we're always here to talk to you, you know that; don't go sitting in this room all day getting morose."

"Thanks Mum."

"Anyway, I've been speaking to the lady in the supplements shop. There were a few extra we needed. She's a nutritionist and she's given me lots of useful advice. We were talking about your special diet; she said if it tastes nice, it's not allowed."

"Wonderful," I said sarcastically. "I really hope it starts to change soon – my diarrhoea is awful. I'm so sorry about the smell every morning."

"That's alright dear. Have you forgotten I've been living with your father for 55 years?!"

I grinned. We could still laugh, always.

I knew already from my friend Gem that the Candida diet was extreme, but eating had lost all joy for me anyway. The fungal infection in my gut that was compromising my immune system was thriving on sugar and causing inflammation throughout my body. I thought back to my birthday and the cake: I'd felt terrible after eating it. Had that and the stress of getting upset triggered the relapse?

I had to avoid refined carbohydrates and yeasts, plus anything sweet at all, even fruit. I would have to scrutinise everything I ate. Mum wrote a list of allowed foods, mainly meats, fish, vegetables and eggs and not much more. Water and coconut milk were allowed but no caffeine or alcohol. I stuck to it religiously.

"She said to take these," said Mum, passing three boxes to me. "Ashwagandha to help your adrenal glands and some milk thistle to help your liver process toxins. Then, this one – oregano oil capsules every morning to kill the Candida."

"I'm rattling with all the tablets now," I said. I silently hoped that all these lotions and potions weren't a waste of time and money. "Pass me that blue pad over there will you, Mum? So I can note these down before I forget."

"This purple one you mean?"

I tutted. Bloody brain fog.

"Right," she continued, "I want you and Dad to get some fresh air on the balcony; I'll put the roast on."

My phone pinged a text from Tom.

Hi love, I hope you are resting up well. Just to let you know that by the time you come back I'll have put up pics of Ferraris and page 3 stunners all over the walls.

I stifled a giggle. God I loved this man.

The September sun was fading and the wisteria had turned from green to yellow on the balcony. I joined Dad and together we gazed out at the hills beyond.

"You alright, Nic?" he asked, sculpting his flat cap firmly on his thinning head and wincing as he stretched his leg.

"Not bad, Dad," I lied.

"Well done girl."

"How are you today?"

"Oh, so so, you know."

I knew that meant he was in awful pain and would prefer to change the subject. His auto-immune disease kept him in a purgatory of torturous pain; his immune system, designed by nature to protect him, had turned against him many years ago following the sudden death of his father.

"It sounds like they're locking down the North East. There's a new wave, cases are doubling there every seven days; sounds pretty grim. That fellow Hancock is inept, totally out of his depth. Only four more U-turns before Christmas."

Talking about the pandemic always made me feel jumpy – as if the news was mimicking my original experience.

"It doesn't sound like we're on top of the numbers at all, does it?" I said, sipping a mint tea and feeling my heartbeat calm a little.

"Quite, it's a mess. They're talking about bringing in tiers for each part of the country. Not sure how that will work, mind. Anyway," he said, rubbing his hands, "There's nothing I like better than looking at the cooked meats from that place in Scotland." He gestured to the brochure on his lap. "It's just arrived! They deliver, you know, all the way down here. Look at that lovely pork shoulder!" he said, his eyes sparkling. "Would you like a look? They also do some excellent sausages."

He must have forgotten I'd been vegetarian before I got ill.

"That's alright Dad, I've got a Saga magazine somewhere."

"I also read there might be a run on mince pies due to the virus this Christmas… very troubling," he tutted. "Any biscuits, Julie?" he called through the glass door.

It had been eight months since I had Covid, and I was now averaging one relapse a month. Every time, I suffered flashbacks of the foetid box room, reliving the panic of the initial infection. My body would repeatedly fire the symptoms back at me: involuntary body shaking, fever, a feeling of intense weight across my whole body like being stretched or squeezed by an incredible pressure from above, and debilitating heart palpitations. Each time my body fared progressively worse, as if the disease was chipping away at my very core, evaporating any reserves I had.

I had to stop the relapses. John had said the current viral presence of Covid was very low, and I believed him. So why was the ghost of Covid haunting me? How could I make it stop? How could I block the appalling messages my body was sending me, and most importantly, where were the messages coming from? I would not stop searching until I knew these answers. *Somebody somewhere knows why this is happening*, I reasoned. I had no idea that the person who knew subconsciously was me.

Back in the lounge, Dad was chatting to his best friend Peter, absent-mindedly twirling his slipper on the end of his foot.

"Oh you know, so so, not too bad. Nic says this flat is where knackered people come to recuperate." He laughed. "Anyway, look squire, about your weekly shop. You want to top yourself up before all those infectious blighters get down there. They're all coming back for university and the first place they'll go is Lidl to do a big trolley full. You need to get in there early, when it's safer. All those millenniums going out and spreading it all around the town."

"I think you mean millennials, dear." Mum winked at me and made a wind-the-call up signal to Dad. He waved her off, wincing and pointing to the phone.

"Alright Pete," he said, "I've got to dash and do this damned order; we'll get some eggs for you mate, yes, no trouble. Cheers for now.

"I do wish you wouldn't do that Julie, talking over me on the phone," he said, feigning ill humour as he loaded up the laptop. "Right then, what do we need, Nic?"

I shuffled in and sat on the leather sofa, not waiting for my breathing to catch up with the movement of my body. "This is what the list says: asparagus is apparently a very good prebiotic for the gut, so we need that. Chard, spinach, seaweed, pumpkin seeds, chia seeds, jicana, and mushrooms but right now I can only have the Shitake kind, other mushrooms can affect the candida apparently," I said, drawing breath.

"Jicana? I've never heard of it. What is it?"

"A root vegetable. I think it's a bit like a potato but tastes more like an apple."

"Most odd. Ok, and how do you spell those mushrooms?" he asked, typing carefully, glasses perched on his nose.

"S.H.I.T..." I grinned, as Mum stood laughing in the doorway.

"Is this a joke?" demanded Dad, a smile slowly breaking through the frown.

"No it isn't! It's pronounced Shit-ah-kay but it's spelt S.H.I.T.A.K.E."

"Sounds like something you get after you've had the jicana," he quipped, his eyes creased as his whole body convulsed with laughter.

We were all laughing now.

Back in my room I tried to rest. I could only manage a couple of hours sitting in a chair, but I found myself anxiously scrolling again. An email had arrived in my inbox telling me my antibody test was negative. My stomach clenched as I read it: I had no protection from reinfection.

Feeling vulnerable, I began googling my symptoms again. My hands felt numb and I felt nauseous and dizzy; my heart pounded most of the day now, and lying down had become unbearable. I had begun sleeping upright in Dad's leather reclining chair, listening to foxes scream outside or watching old sitcoms.

A part of my lower back ached, which I assumed was my kidneys. I had researched enough by now to know that some of my symptoms pointed to chronic vitamin B12 deficiency, but I was in an impossible situation. My blood tests had come back normal, so the GPs at my surgery were refusing to give me the injection I so desperately needed. I remembered what John had said about serum tests for vitamin B12 being notoriously flawed. They only check for what is flowing through the needle at a given point in time, but they need to check what the body is doing with the B12: it needs to be getting to the tissues and organs to be effective. I had hit a brick wall. I couldn't face more waiting on hold, endless repetition of my case history and predictable frustrating responses: *I'm sorry there is no evidence for that, your levels of vitamin are in the supranormal range. You have plenty of B12 in your blood.* I popped another B12 under my tongue; my symptoms receded almost immediately but I knew it would be temporary.

I had to tell Mum about my cancer screening appointment. The lump was hard and pronounced, like a small marble under the skin. How do you find the words to give your mother more worry? *I am my parents' worst nightmare,* I thought. But my mum is strong and I knew she'd be practical. I also knew we'd have to hide it from Dad, for the moment anyway.

I remembered his charismatic father of the bride speech. Brimming with pride, he'd described me as 'stoic', recounting the time I'd skidded across the road on my bicycle in the rain, yards from the bumper of a Routemaster bus on Westminster Bridge Road. As the four-way traffic had come to an abrupt halt, I'd gazed up from the tarmac at stunned faces staring at me in horror through murky bus windows. I hadn't told my parents at the time, but when they'd seen the crack on my helmet, I'd eventually come clean.

Stoic was a more accurate description of Dad, though. He was the indomitable one, coping with debilitating rheumatoid arthritis for more than fifty years, which had ravaged his joints. I had seldom heard him complain. He was always reticent to ask for help and would rather struggle on, often in agonising pain. In comparison, I felt far from stoic; I was a burden, their helpless baby again. I didn't identify with the marginalised person I had become, nor as a sick person with an unknown disease. I was a wife, mum, friend, daughter.

Forcing the negative thoughts from my mind, I resolved to stay positive. I turned off all the media from my phone: I'd had enough bad news in this flat, I didn't need to add a diet of daily statistics and hospital updates to my panicked brain.

I called Mum in. Dad was in the lounge, watching *Dad's Army*.

"Mum, can you have a look in my bag, there's something I need you to read." She knew from my conspiratorial tone to close the door. I was taking the easy way out but I couldn't say the words. I felt like I was constantly hurting her. I scanned her eyes as she opened the envelope and read the words on the page. *NHS Breast Unit*.

"I'm sorry, Mum," I began, "I've got a lump. It's quite big, or at least it's pronounced. I can only feel it when I turn on my side but it's there. I saw the doctor and she's referred me to the clinic. The appointment is next week. I've been checking the Long Covid Facebook group and some other women have it, so I'm hoping it's benign and just another symptom." I winced, waiting for her response.

"You don't have cancer," she said firmly, "you're going to be fine. I'm sure this is nothing to worry about, but let's not tell your father, he won't be able to cope."

It was just how I'd thought she'd respond. Strong, positive, as she always is.

Another impossible situation presented itself.

"Mum, I'm worried I might have to have a biopsy. If I do and it gets infected, I won't be able to fight off the infection because my immune system is compromised. Then if that happens I will have to take antibiotics which will destroy what little progress I've made on my microbiome."

I remembered that antibiotic means 'anti-life' and that some antibiotics kill both the good and bad bacteria in the gut. I bitterly regretted the times I'd taken antibiotics for sniffles and sore throats, or earaches that would have healed without intervention.

"Listen," she replied, "you've jumped about five steps forward, let's take one step at a time shall we? No one can predict the future. I remember when you were at university, I found a lump. I went on my own to the clinic and didn't tell a soul. I cried all the way there, but it was fine."

She stood up. "It's important that we get it checked out. We'll tell Dad you're going to have a chest X-ray for Covid, which isn't too far off the truth. I'm an optimist, your father is the opposite, he catastrophizes so we'll spare him this one. Do try to get some rest now and don't let this play on your mind – you need to try and stay stress free."

We're doomed, doomed I tell you! boomed Private Fraser from the lounge.

Chapter 8

The Empty Gauge

The digital clock on the DVD player was blinking 3:43am. I was bolt upright in Dad's leather recliner, startled awake by the strangest of visions. I had been viewing a fuel gauge in my mind's eye. An energy accumulator, my body battery. It was dropping dangerously fast and emergency warning signs were flashing. As the arrow on the gauge approached the red zone, I woke to the desperate pounding of my heart – a familiar terror, only this time it was different.

This time, my body was crashing on empty. Desperate, I popped two vitamin B12 under my tongue. Then two more. How many could I take, I wondered? What was an overdose? I knew that people with chronic B12 deficiency needed injections every day. I also knew the condition was life threatening. My body was shutting down. I could feel my kidneys groaning beneath my skin. That shadowy room of doors flashed into my mind's eye again: the closing of another exit door, me on the floor, incarcerated in an infinite vault of nothing and everything, the clink of the padlock securing my imprisonment.

I endured the torturous situation as long as I could, watching shadows creeping up the walls and disappearing into the high cornicing. Minutes ticked slowly by. I wondered about calling an ambulance, but how critical was I? When could I alert my parents of my desperate state?

5:40am. 5:50am. I wondered if my heart would stop in the chair. I couldn't bear the thought of them finding me. My heart was the map to my future; it couldn't fail. Not now, not yet.

They were sleeping now with the door open, in case I called in the night. I managed to shuffle off the seat and hobbled to the hallway door.

"Mum, I croaked, clutching my chest. "I think I'm having a heart attack."

The early morning street lights were blinking on as we sped towards the hospital. Dad drove me as close as possible to the entrance, and I put on my mask as Mum wheeled me through the doors. I begged her to leave as I knew infections were rising rapidly every day. Reluctantly, she left me to register.

The receptionist took my details and a porter pushed me into triage. There I waited passively in Dad's wheelchair. Looking down at my skeletal frame, my lined hands hanging limply in my lap, I felt old, way beyond my years. Nearby, menacing machines blurred, buzzed and twitched. I looked up at the cracked, tessellated panel of ceiling tiles that bulged to reveal the electrical wiring above. The stark strip-lighting stung my eyes and my vision blurred. My brain was hypervigilant but my body was weak, and there was a throbbing in my ears.

I heard the triage nurse bustle by, stopping to chat to the receptionist across the aisle. He was reviewing my notes with disdain.

"Is she wearing a mask?" he frowned. "Well, what does she

want us to do about Long Covid? What is she doing here?"

A muffled response.

He tutted under his mask.

As I sat in my wheelchair in the tiny room, his colleague took my pulse and wired me up to an ECG machine. A crushing despair welled up inside me and I felt wholly insignificant. They thought I was a phoney with a sham disease, that I was feigning my illness. But surely they could see how ill I was? *I must get my injection,* I thought. The nurse looked at the read-out of the ECG and my blood pressure.

"I can see you are tachycardic, but I'm not too worried about that."

Well, I bloody am, I thought. *You try living with this.* I felt a deep sense of disempowerment, like an injured child craving the support of an emotionally detached mother.

"I need a B12 injection," I said, "my kidneys feel like they are failing; everything hurts."

"Where are you feeling the kidney pain?"

What, was this a test? Does she think I'm making this up, or am I being paranoid? Is she genuinely trying to help? "Lower back."

"Do you have a positive Covid test?"

"There were none available in March." I sighed, wondering how many times I'd answered that question in the last seven months.

"I'll speak to the consultant on duty," she said, getting up from her chair, "but I don't think we'll be able to help you as it's not an acute issue. It's likely that you'll need to speak to your GP."

Her voice had taken on a shadowy, distant tone, but nonetheless it penetrated my soul. Intense heat flushed my face. There it was again, the concentric circle of emotions generated by my illness, radiating from my core. Shame and anger followed by frustration and fear. I hesitated to tell her how many times I'd already spoken to GPs about my vitamin deficiency. Inside I was screaming, but all I could manage was a consensual nod. Even so, I was becoming more resolute. *I'm not leaving until I get my B12 injection,* I thought. This time, my fight-or-flight was helping me: I was in survival mode and I would not stop until they listened.

Minutes passed. The nurse opened the door and clicked it shut behind her.

"The consultant says this is a new incident, so they will admit you to the ward."

My relief was palpable; I had a foot in the door.

A porter came to usher me into a ward. I counted the seven cubicles. It was a snapshot of emergency life being played out during a pandemic. The nurse on duty looked exhausted: a trickle of sweat ran from her temple down the side of her mask; she brushed it back with her gloved hand. A man opposite was having a catheter fitted. Two cubicles down, an obstreperous woman with dementia was repeatedly launching herself out of bed and crashing onto the floor, holding her bruised head and ripping off her mask, assaulting the ward with a torrent of high-pitched wailing. There was a low, guttural groan coming from somewhere near the exit doors. It was like a manifestation of the underworld; heat rising from beneath the depths of the earth, every soul present being punished for their sins, awaiting the assessment foretelling oblivion or salvation. I lay in anticipation of the judgement for what seemed like an interminable time.

A staff nurse and a trainee doctor pulled back the screen.

"Hi," said the nurse, "I'm Claire and this is Lara. I've been reading your notes. It sounds like you've been through a really tough time." Her voice was kind.

"Yes," I said. "I've had to move out of my home with my children and husband and move in with my parents due to Long Covid." I explained how badly I needed the B12 injection and that my body wasn't distributing the B12 to the right areas of my body, even though I had enough in my bloods. I used every ounce of strength I had to give the best possible account of my situation. This was the time to fight my corner.

She listened intently and seemed shocked at my story.

"You're very thin," she said.

"I'm not absorbing nutrients properly; I've got digestive problems."

"Okay. Lara is going to do a few reflex tests, a blood test and then I'll speak to the consultant and see what we can do for you. The blood tests will go to the lab here on site so they'll be back soon."

The young student doctor tapped hesitantly at my knees and arms with a rubber hammer, checking my responses and looking in my eyes under the instruction of her more experienced colleague.

"You're doing really well," I whispered. She smiled nervously. I could tell she was worried she wasn't doing it all in the right order. I thought about my daughters and wondered what profession they would go into. I wondered if I would live to see them finish education and begin working, and my heart ached as once again I imagined a life without them, and their life without me.

They took the bloods and left, promising to return with the doctor on duty. I spent the hours that passed tracing the lines on the tiled ceiling and listening to anguished auxiliaries as they tried to stop the lady in bed nine from crashing to the floor.

Finally they returned, apologising on behalf of the consultant doctor who'd been called to another emergency.

"Your results have come back and there is plenty of B12 in your bloods," she said. "But the doctor has reviewed your case and because of your symptoms, he's agreed you should have the injection. It will be intramuscular, so into your thigh muscle. It should last three months. Is that okay?"

I burst into tears. Relief coursed through my body.

"I'm sorry I can't hug you," she said, with deep empathy and an expression that showed her frustration with the situation. "We have the vitamin in the pharmacy so we'll put a call out and it should be with you within the hour. Chantelle will administer that for you." She indicated to the young nurse standing at the nearby station. "You'll also be referred to ambulatory care as an outpatient and you may be able to speak to a neurologist there if you would like to. Bye, now – I hope it helps you make a full recovery."

They pulled back the screen and headed over to the man with the catheter. I was humbled by their resilience, empathy and duty of care; they were a million miles away from the triage team.

Chantelle was encouraging Mavis back into her bed repeatedly. I could just make out the bruising on Mavis' face, a deep purple covering a bulbous eye. A red plastic file had been delivered and was tantalisingly close, on the mobile station just beyond my cubicle. I knew it was my injection. I was totally fixated on it, but had to wait another agonising hour until Mavis was secured. Again, I stared at the ceiling and tried to block out the racing of my heart.

I must have closed my eyes momentarily. When I opened them again, Chantelle was standing over me.

"Alright sweet," she said, "this one's for you. Sorry about the delay, I couldn't leave that lady on her own."

"No problem."

"So this will be going into your muscle on your left leg. If I can just find..."

I rolled down my pyjamas, feeling a tinge of body shame as her gloved hands struggled to find enough muscle mass to inject into. She pinched the skin roughly together and the needle went in.

"It can take 24 to 78 hours to take full effect," she advised. But as she was talking, I felt the instantaneous hit of B12 as it flooded through my tissues. Legs tingling from top to bottom, it was as if all the cells in my lower body were jolted into action. The pains in my legs receded.

"You can go home now. I'll call a porter to wheel you to the exit."

Chapter 9

Nervous Breakthrough

A week passed of better days and bad days. Progress wasn't linear. I always felt like I was lurching from one alarming symptom to another. Although the B12 injection helped, chronic pain still gripped my arms and legs; my body was prone to internal vibrating and the insomnia was debilitating. But there were gains, too: my digestion was slowly starting to improve and I no longer had pain in my abdomen on digesting foods. I'd progressed from being so ill I could barely speak or even move, to being able to spend a little more time on the sofa than in bed. This was progress, and in the midst of all the pain, I could feel my spark coming back. I heard the familiar whirr of the printer as Dad switched off the lunchtime news. We'd agreed that from now on I would stop watching the headlines and delete all my social media apps. It felt like a release. I eased off the bed and stepped into the lounge. He was sitting in his favourite chair, laptop on his knees, and as I sat he passed me the latest update from John:

Nicola has been taking the supplements for two weeks now and I have dowsed all of her numbers again. I'm pleased to say the majority of things have responded, though obviously a way to go in certain areas. Continue taking the supplements as she has been for a while longer, but add in daily the following:

Vitamin K2 (2 a day with food) and Swanson PQQ (1 day with food), plus G&G amino acid blend, (1 a day on rising empty stomach) wait 45 minutes before eating. It is always good to have a broad spectrum along with the L-Methionine.

You can see why I didn't suggest she take everything at once, but she is clearly in a better place to deal with this now. I am a bit wary of reducing supplements too soon though, it can seriously hinder any process you have made.

As far as my results go, pretty much all the nutrient levels you have been supplementing are approaching normality but need to be held there. Some very low general indicators have improved as follows (new/old):

Overall vitality	(35%/0%)
Immune system function	(70%/30%)
Neural network function	(90%/40%)
Muscle function	(30%/10%)
Digestive group function	(45%/10%)
Nervous system function	(60%/10%)

So still a way to go but I'm pleased we have got this far so soon and it appears you are too. Let's hope it continues but don't be in a rush. You've been in a very bad way for a long time and we're only two weeks in!

Best wishes

John

"Well that all sounds encouraging," said Dad cheerily. "Although I have no idea what an amino acid is – do you, Nic?"

I shook my head and began to search it up. I was starting to be able to use a laptop for short periods without feeling ill – but it was difficult to stop once I'd started, which often resulted in a relapse of symptoms.

"So it says here, 'Amino acids are compounds that play many critical roles in your body. They're needed for vital processes like the building of proteins and synthesis of hormones and neurotransmitters.'"

"I think the improved 'neural network' figure explains why I feel I can concentrate for longer," I said.

"Yes but don't overdo it!" warned Mum. Mum's role was to keep us both grounded, and she was extremely good at it.

Now that I was feeling slightly stronger, I was desperate to learn more about my illness. I knew a cure was out there, I just needed to understand what was wrong with me.

My blood pressure was still disturbingly high when I tried to stand, and after eating. Even though I barely slept I never felt tired. I took out my compact and looked at my face. Why didn't I have dark circles under my eyes? It's impossible to sleep three hours a night for four months and not be tired, surely? My body must be flooded with adrenaline, I reasoned, which was stopping me sleeping.

I used what little strength I had to research more. I stumbled across a post on the Facebook group about therapies people were using to calm their racing heartbeats. Many of us were reporting similar symptoms by now: tachycardia or 'POTS', numb hands, internal vibrating, hair loss, sickness, diarrhoea, depression, back pain… the list went on. I tried not to check the Facebook posts too often to protect my fragile mental health — the stories were distressing to read. Many of us were being ignored, or worse, gaslit by the medical profession. People were leaving their partners to fend for themselves; some, like me, were bedridden. Mothers were unable to look after their children, many were suffering from undiagnosed and terrifying symptoms that changed daily. Hard as it was being separated from Tom and the girls, I was deeply thankful for my supportive family.

One post on the group stood out. It was about vagus nerve stimulation: people were taking cold showers and getting temporary respite from symptoms. I'd heard about the vagus nerve from taking yoga classes in the past. Known as the wandering nerve, it helps regulate the nervous system. Maybe if I could find out what it did in the body, I could start using vagus nerve stimulation therapies to try and heal myself.

I found a video explainer about the vagus nerve – but it was about an hour long. Desperate to watch it, I also knew I didn't have the strength.

"Dad," I called through the open door.

"Yes love?"

An hour later, Dad called me into the lounge. He looked excited.

"Well, that was fascinating! I'd never heard of the vagus nerve before, but it turns out it's very important in regulating virtually every part of your body. It might even help with my arthritis pain, actually. And it seems it's also important for you because it regulates your autonomic nervous system. The guy on there was saying that if you can stimulate it, it can help with many problems like digestive things, your heart, lungs, and other functions like sense of smell and swallowing. It's even important for the acidity level in your stomach which helps you break down food. He says people in constant stress states are going to struggle with these things because the vagus nerve is not being stimulated."

My mind was working fast. "I wonder if that's why people with Long Covid are getting anosmia – lack of sense of smell?"

Dad nodded and tapped his notepad. "I made some notes here because I couldn't remember it all. He talks about what happens when you're in fight-or-flight mode: your body sends more blood to the muscles so you can get ready to run, digestion slows down and you lose your appetite. It can involve all the muscles in the body. Your blood pressure rises because it has to pump blood through these tense muscles. When you're in this state your body feels as though its survival is threatened. You're ready to run for your life.

"He says this is a fear state – the body is mobilised and that comes when we don't feel safe. The problem with fear is you get into a sort of fear loop and it becomes energised. Then you start to get the sort of problems you've got, because you can't shut it down."

"I completely agree about the fear thing," called Mum through the kitchen hatch. "You got yourself into a hell of a state at the start of the pandemic, worrying about everyone. Constantly reading the news, looking at statistics, endless stress, just like your father. I knew that wasn't good for you."

"I do wish you wouldn't interrupt, Julie," tutted Dad. "Anyway, this fellow also talks about the nerves and the skeleton and how they are so interconnected. He says along with the vagus nerve, we use four other cranial nerves to regulate the nervous system. You can see here," he continued, jabbing his pen at a diagram of a human spine on the computer screen.

"This nerve is called the CNXI," he said, pointing to an image of the skull. "That nerve and the dysfunction of the vagus nerve often go together, apparently."

"Maybe that's why I have neck and back pains," I said. I thought back to the creeping, aching pains in my skeleton, my neck, ears and my lower back. I had thought it was due to vitamin deficiency, but it wasn't going away. I'd also noticed I could barely rotate my neck without increasing my heartbeat to a frightening rate.

"Exactly. From the sounds of this, your doctors should be looking at your nervous system as he says it's a factor in many diseases. "What's also interesting is he says the vagus nerve is affected by your breathing pattern. Basically, if you're not breathing properly, then the vagus nerve struggles to do its job. Didn't you say your breathing was really laboured with Covid?"

"Yes, I was breathing in a really shallow way for weeks afterwards. I had to work very hard to learn to breathe again from the diaphragm, instead of mouth breathing."

"So maybe that also affected the fight-or-flight response in your spine, because your body was sending out incorrect messages that you're still in danger. The vagus nerve also acts as a temperature gauge to control your heart rate. He talks about that Phos Choline stuff you're taking as being very important in regulating the heart and also for your muscles to prevent fatigue."

"Which could explain my weird temperature regulation, the racing heartbeat…"

"And listen to this: 'Chronic fight-or-flight can trigger your adrenal glands to produce high amounts of stress hormones such as cortisol which can push the body into adrenal fatigue.'"

"But that's exactly what I have!" I exclaimed. "I get adrenaline rushes, it's like being in a car crash but there isn't actually anything happening to me. I'm so easily startled, it's horrible. I expect I've got adrenal fatigue as well."

Mum had come in from the kitchen. "You probably have Nic," she said. "But don't worry, these things will get fixed in time; healing is not linear, remember. The body is amazing at healing itself."

Dad continued. "He also says when your vagus nerve isn't working properly, toxins can build up because the right messages aren't being delivered or received in the brain that tell the body to heal itself. And you know you thought you had Herpes? Well that's probable, too – it seems a virus like Covid can weaken the immune system allowing old viruses to crop up again. He says vagus nerve malfunction can mean chronic inflammation – that's important for me with my arthritis. Maybe I should be doing some of these techniques myself."

"The body's so complex," I said, "I can't believe I didn't know any of this."

"Me neither, but why would you?" said Dad. "Most of these things happen without us thinking about it."

"So how do I get my vagus nerve working? If that's going to help me get well?" I rubbed my temples and yawned.

"She's getting overtired Malc, let's talk about it later."

“No, no,” I said, sitting upright, “this is important. I need to know this.”

“You have to increase your vagal tone,” said Dad. “I’m not sure what that means exactly but it seems it’s restoring the balance, and that will help you recover more quickly. There are lots of ways to do it, some of them you are already doing.” He looked down at his hastily scribbled notes. “Meditation, singing, humming, cold water showers, slow breathing, laughter, smelling essential oils… According to this, dabbing oils behind your ear is about the closest you can get to stimulating the nerve directly as it’s so close to that area of the neck.”

“Wow Dad, it’s like you’ve done a degree on the human body. Thank you for doing this for me.”

I thought about my upcoming outpatient appointment with ambulatory care with excitement. I made a mental note to raise the vagus nerve with the neurologist. I instinctively felt that vagal tone was integral to my recovery.

“I never imagined your father extolling the benefits of aromatherapy with you,” laughed Mum, “this year has certainly turned everything on its head. He’ll be giving up pork pies next.”

“Not a chance!’ shot back Dad, laughing. “Have we got any in, actually Julie? I’m ready for a spot of lunch.”

Chapter 10

Disease Begins In The Gut

I blinked as Mum pulled back the curtains and let the morning light flood in. The magnificent horse chestnut next door had begun to shed its lime-green cases revealing mahogany-bright conkers, like glinting gems of autumn. The seasons were changing, the world continued to turn. I was still stuck in my frail body, yearning for freedom, to be outside myself, a free spirit, function without broken form.

I swallowed the first tablets of the day and took a swig of water. The night had been gruelling. Palpitations had ripped me from deep sleep whenever I moved my neck. I had taken to wearing a neck brace. I remembered hearing about animals in the wild that couldn't rotate their necks fully to escape from predators. They were the ones who inevitably died first. Natural selection.

My appointment with the neurologist had gone badly. Anger bubbled up as I remembered his dismissive attitude. I'd felt intimidated. He'd ridiculed my suggestions of stimulating the vagus nerve, calling them dangerous and suggesting I could induce a stroke. Then he diagnosed me as having panic attacks. Why would I have panic attacks on holiday when I was at my most restful and happy? It just didn't make sense. This was not some psychosomatic disorder, a mental health cry for help or an imaginary illness. John had mentioned chronic fatigue sufferers in the 1980s being dismissed and ignored, scathingly referred to as having yuppy flu, or worse, being stupid or lazy. These wretched people were prescribed antidepressants and sleeping tablets. Why had we not learned anything in thirty years? I was bitterly frustrated. I looked like a walking corpse – couldn't he see how ill I was? I had climbed into the car in a rage, denouncing the appointment as a total waste of time and energy. The sad truth was that by now I had extremely low expectations of conventional medicine.

I tried to push back the tears as I scanned my phone for the latest update from John. I was desperate for good news about my recovery. Mum had promised me that I would get better, but she didn't know for sure any more than I did. She was good at what Dad would refer to as 'rallying the troops' and keeping morale high, but I knew she hid her concern from me. She would not admit any kind of weakness – that would mean giving in to my disease and her role was to radiate positivity and avert hysteria at all costs. But I'd noticed her blotchy eyes, only part-hidden beneath her glasses, the telltale rashy skin of distress; no one was an emotional vacuum. Sometimes being strong is showing your weakness.

Hello Nicola

So sorry to hear you are still unwell but I think in fact it may help in getting to the bottom of this.

On reflection, when I dowsed you on 12th September there

were 42 results that were pretty terrible and as you know that presented a great problem of where to start! There has clearly been progress and that is reflected in the fact that I now have only a few results of concern and you say you feel you have improved a lot since we started so let's keep trying.

The results of concern are as follows:

- Overall vitality: started at zero on 12th Sept, rose to 35% and is still 35%, should be 80+%
- Digestive function: started at 10% on 12th Sept, since stuck around 40%, ideally 80+%
- Nervous system function: started at 10%, stuck around 50%, should be 80+%
- Muscle function: started at 10%, now 40% should be 80+%

So despite these numbers I believe we are now in a position to look at phase two of your recovery – that is, your gut health. There was clearly a gut imbalance before you had Covid and the COV-2 virus made it much worse. The special diet you have been on will have helped manage the Candida infection and you are evidently now able to absorb at least some of the nutrients you are taking.

You are right to draw attention to the vagus nerve, it is the main communication channel between the gut and the brain. Stimulation of the vagus nerve is required and that makes sense, because the message that 'everything is ok, nutrients are available' has to come from the gut via the vagus nerve. The allopathic medicine system takes no real account of the gut microbiome, which is rather incredible since for every message the brain sends to the gut, the gut sends about ten to the brain! Since microbiome research really took off around the year 2000, many leading scientists believe gut health is the number one factor in just about every disease, bearing in mind that 70% of the immune system is in the gut. However I am told that on average it takes at least 17 years for the science to turn up in a doctor's office, often much longer. There are many specialised tests you can do on the gut but they are expensive; it may be something to look at down the line for you.

It's early days but I am leaning more towards a gut problem rather than the malfunctioning of the vagus nerve. However, that should not in any way discourage you from doing vagus nerve-related yoga exercises and breathing, and it is good to hear you have the motivation and ability to do so. Again, an indicator of progress.

Your Vitamin B12 situation is strange to say the least and I think I will need to do further research on what is happening here. It seems that Covid can cause an issue with the malabsorption of B12 via the ileum; I can see you are taking in enough of the vitamin, but your body is not using it effectively.

The B12 in food is broken down in the stomach (by hydrochloric acid and protease) and needs Intrinsic factor to complete that. I did not find a problem with your Intrinsic factor, though it is a well recognised issue. What I did find was a problem with your level of stomach acid (low) and with chlorine (hence chlorides) also very low.

I believe that you are not breaking down the B12 from food sufficiently well for it to be absorbed and hence you were heavily dependent on the sublingual dose you had been taking before the injection, which goes direct to the bloodstream. The level of chlorine was initially +1, it is ideally +8 but had dropped to -9 at the end of September. This type of behaviour is very common. Things that appear okay or normal to start with can suddenly drop once other things in short supply are replenished. My take on that is the body has previously made little demands on things but once it does they drop like a stone.

I checked for stomach acidity and it is indeed low (+1, usually +9). That might explain two things: the shortage of chlorine in the form of hydrochloride, and an inability to break up any B12 you get from diet, into a form that can be absorbed later in the gut. Folate is also involved but you have corrected that (was -8, now +8). It's likely stress has been a factor at play here: chronic stress can seriously affect gut regulation in general and in particular acidity and it's clear you've been exposed to significant sustained trauma.

So, I have suggested you get some betaine hydrochloride to bring your stomach acidity up to where it needs to be and take one with each meal. It's also worth trying to eat some quality lamb's liver once or twice a week if you can tolerate it, as it's an excellent source of B12 and iron.

I would also suggest taking some L-Glutamine powder: take two teaspoons in a glass of water before breakfast and two teaspoons before tea. The L-Glutamine helps calm the gut; it is an amino acid that helps maintain the intestinal wall. You have problems with leaky gut; you have an increased permeability of the gut lining which is allowing toxins and bacteria to enter the bloodstream causing chronic inflammation. As the gut is a major organ associated with immune function, it could make you more susceptible to developing autoimmune diseases, so it's very important for you to heal your stomach wall.

Let's hope we can look at backing off a few supplements in the next couple of weeks. It's always preferable to pick things up via your diet. Once we have made some progress it will be a good idea to focus on your gut biome, but we'll talk about that later.

Best regards

John

"Liver!" I grimaced. "Ew, no thanks."

"Your father will be pleased," said Mum, "he loves my liver and onions."

"I know it's important and I've started eating red meat, but liver, really? Offal? I just don't know if I can bear it."

"Well do you want to get better or not? Just try some, it's yummy with gravy and mash. Delicious!"

I agreed, reluctantly.

I finished my breakfast and reread the email in an attempt to hold the information in my foggy brain. I now had a plan and was project managing my recovery. I felt more empowered. My vitamin levels were holding. I was managing to eat more; I was still painfully thin but allowed myself to hope that things very slowly were starting to improve.

Mum came back in. "Now," she said, "it's a beautiful day and not too cold yet… I think we should go out. I know you have to be careful, but why don't we go to the botanical gardens? I can push you around the path, there are lots of benches and hopefully it won't be too busy."

"I can't bear the thought of being in that sickly chariot," I said, miserably. "The *does she take sugar* brigade will be out patronising the hell out of me. Dad says everyone treats him as if he was gaga in the wheelchair. I'd rather just sit on the balcony."

"Nonsense. You need some fresh air. We'll go as soon as we're ready."

I gathered my bobble hat, gloves, coat and phone and sat waiting for my parents. The slightest activity was still causing my heart to thump but I did feel stronger. Perhaps I really could manage a few steps around the park? I knew we needed to get out now while we still could: it looked like we would be locking down again soon and the botanical gardens would be closed to visitors. Back in April we'd been promised a return to normality in November, but here we were again, case numbers spiralling.

Dad had been a wheelchair user for years and I now clearly understood his frustration. You become invisible. People look right through the chair as if it's glass and direct questions to the person pushing. Even political correctness had not reached most people when it came to interactions with the wheelchair community.

The air was crisp and the sky was bright but blustery as we navigated the paths around the gardens. We looked a strange sight, all masked in the open air, Dad with his two sticks and Mum pushing her middle-aged daughter, blankets on her knees. I caught snatches of glossy information signs on the bark of the trees: Ilanthus Altissima, the Tree of Heaven – the tallest in the UK. We stopped momentarily under a stately oak. I gazed up into its branches as they creaked and waved wildly, marvelling at its strength, its still core, rooted and firm.

I felt wretched and old before my time.

"Someone's coming!" yelled Dad, panic catching in his throat, "Get back Julie, keep your mask up!"

"ALRIGHT MALC, no need to make a fuss."

"Get in Julie, get IN," he hissed, scuttling on his sticks as fast as he could to the opposite bank.

A grey-haired man with a flat cap and mask covering only his mouth was making his way briskly towards us. I groaned inwardly. *Please don't chat to us.* I didn't need an octogenarian consoling me on the terrible hand fate had played me.

"Lovely day!" he boomed.

Pulling my hat down and collar up, I tried to hide under the blanket. *Please don't speak to me,* I prayed.

"And how are YOU today?"

To my horror, he was making a point of speaking to me directly. I cringed. He hadn't got the memo, he was supposed to be ignoring the disabled person. *Oh god, make it stop.*

"Fine," I managed, willing Mum to keep pushing.

"She's not normally in a wheelchair, this is temporary," Mum said, trying to be helpful as I flushed a deep crimson.

The man moved off in the direction of the rose garden.

I was fuming. Not only are you a prisoner in your own body, but you're forced to participate in humiliating conversations that you cannot influence. Or worse, a conversation goes on over your head and you're not only uninvited but ignored. This was exactly what I had hoped to avoid. I remembered Mum recounting the tale of their Caribbean cruise. On the first night, they'd been invited to the Captain's table amid great fanfare, and Mum had been seated next to the Captain's wife. As the wine was poured the Captain's wife remarked on how much she loved coming on cruises with her husband, despite there being so many *disabled* people onboard. Mum interrupted her saying she must find out where her husband was. She re-joined the table moments later pushing Dad in his wheelchair, eyeballing the Captain's wife who had now turned an evidently mortified shade of puce.

"Do you mind if we go home now? I'm getting a bit cold," I lied. I had endured enough absurd humiliation for one day. I felt ashamed and worthless, a non human. I wanted to shut myself off from humanity and hide from the world.

Back at the flat I lay on the bed exhausted, angry and frustrated. The anger was like a current of energy flowing through me. I was not willing to accept the diagnosis of Long Covid. I thought of the oak tree buffeted by the storm, its foundation unyielding. I would find my reserves of strength. I would fight. I would choose a new future for myself. If no doctors were going to save me, I would have to save myself. I had already come so far; I would battle on.

I thought back to my first A&E visit: the hurried goodbye note I'd written for Tom and the children. It had been woefully lacking in sentiment. If I were them I would have felt cheated and angry on receiving it. How can you put a lifetime of feeling, hopes and dreams into a few paragraphs? How can you explain the profundity of a mother's love – is it still there from beyond the grave?

In the lounge, Dad was playing 'Lark Ascending'. I looked out at the countryside beyond. The music seemed to encapsulate the stillness of the earth: a divine meditation before breaking free, transcendent, soaring skyward. The theme of the melody was not lost on me. Was I about to take flight? I willed every cell in my body to listen and believe.

Chapter 11

Thoughts Become Matter

As September turned to October I spent the days exploring new ways to stimulate my vagus nerve comfortably with the low energy levels that I had. There were plenty of examples online and I was at my happiest being able to research every inch of the web for information. My cancer biopsy had come back negative. The doctor had told me it was a completely benign lump often caused by stress or trauma. On some level I felt a modicum of relief: at least I could concentrate on recovering from only one serious illness and not two.

My routine became a bizarre ritual of chanting, cold face washes, laughter yoga, deep slow breathing and gargling. In the early days of my acute disease I'd practised deep breathing to help my lungs recover, and I'd kept this up. Proper breathing was crucial to circulation in my lymphatic system, which needed to work much harder than usual to drain all the toxins away. Breathwork also helped control my heart rate, and although it was still a struggle, I was managing more days out of bed.

Happily, Dad was always pleased to watch comedies with me and was well known for his roaring laughter and dancing eyes when retelling a good joke. I would watch sitcoms on repeat and when I did, the pain in my legs faded away. I seemed to be changing my internal chemistry when I laughed. My emotional state was evidently sending a message to my cells; was I turning off the genes that were causing me chronic pain, or turning on healthy genes without pain, or both?

I knew by now that I had dysautonomia, the dysregulation of the autonomic nervous system; I knew very little about it and dearly hoped it was reversible. My nervous system still couldn't regulate my heart's response to exertion of any kind: even moving from sitting to standing sent my heart rate soaring.

I longed to see my children; it had been nearly four weeks. I comforted myself by sending them quirky pictures on our group WhatsApp. I came to dread the weekly Facetime with the girls: the exertion exhausted me and seeing them on a screen reminded me of the pain of separation. I preferred to suppress those emotions to prevent them overwhelming me. Lily had completed half term at her new school and I hadn't been there to support her. Had she made new friends? Was she struggling, happy or sad? And Ella's GCSE choices would need to be made soon. My rightful place was with them, right now, to help them through their life journey. I imagined their life without me.

The illness had stopped me communicating with my children, and my whole social circle. But then, wasn't everyone locked away anyway? *I'm not missing anything*, I reasoned. We're all in our bubbles, on our own, in our own heads. What was this isolation doing to all of us mentally? How damaging was this enforced imprisonment? I pictured thousands of lonely people all over Britain sitting in front of an electric fire with only the television with all its unchecked, unfolding horror for company.

I struggled to shower and barely had the muscle strength to hold up my arms long enough to wash my hair. The plastic fold-down shower seat was a godsend, as I could rest while washing. I marvelled at the disabled paraphernalia in the flat: I'd never really noticed it before but it fostered independence for me now. *They should make these shower seats more stylish*, I thought; *every home should have one.*

Nights were still extremely tough and debilitating relapses came sporadically, causing my legs to shake and my heart to pound. My legs and arms were frequently flushed with chronic inflammation. These symptoms almost felt like second nature, an addictive habit of subconscious self-flagellation with an unknown cause. My body seemed to be trying to compensate by releasing surges of adrenaline in a fruitless attempt to correct my ailing heart. It felt like a civil war was raging within me, with my adrenal glands on the verge of collapse.

At my lowest points in the long, dark nights of broken sleep, I feared I would die. I wondered if my diseased heart would just stop beating. Still, I refused to stop fighting. I would not accept that there was no cure for Long Covid. They said it was 'incurable': I thought about the word and broke it down. In-cure-able. Maybe that meant I could cure it from within?

I had thought physicians were the only authority on healing; I had been socially conditioned to expect the medical profession to revive me. That's their job – but what if they don't have the knowledge? That's not their fault, but neither did that mean the answers didn't exist and couldn't be found.

I chose not to waste valuable energy feeling bitter, and not to blame anyone else. John had said early on, *we have to take responsibility for our own healing.* I understood this now. I'd been too passive for too long. If I wanted to live, the responsibility lay with me. This illness was the result of my own conduct, although it had been beyond my conscious awareness. The physical and emotional stress I had put my body under had negatively influenced every part of my body, creating chemical stress, I could see that now. I now had to positively influence my body to heal – outsourcing my recovery was not an option. I didn't know if the vagus nerve work would cure my dysautonomia. My future was unknown and in that way all of us are alike. We may be in different places right now, but we all have unknown futures.

One night I was lying awake, desperately scrolling through my phone in search of answers. I was searching for recovery from chronic fatigue as I had done many times, but on this occasion, I stumbled across a YouTube clip of a company in Australia that claimed to help cure ME-type symptoms. I watched the video advertising their company and explaining the techniques they used. I heard the word *visualisation*, rewound and played the 20-second clip again to try and understand more about what they were saying.

We use a combination of visualisations and ANS rewire to help heal our patients.

ANS rewire by now I knew was autonomic nervous system rewire… but what were visualisations? I was desperate to understand what that meant, but the information was locked behind a paywall for their services. The word was all I had to go on.

I thought about what visualisations could mean in this

context. I knew that Olympians, cyclists and downhill skiers used mental imagery to improve their chances of winning: the faster they could imagine themselves doing something, the more success they had in their sport. But could that help me recover from illness? *Could I think myself well?*

I began to explore other examples online of where visualisations had helped with healing. To my amazement, there were many stories of how the brain could help cure the body, from depression and alcoholism to bulimia, even cancers. How had I never known about this? A way forward was opening up: I would imagine myself recovering.

I had a vivid imagination, but I'd also need stamina and clarity of mind. I'd have to learn how to remove existing negative memories to make way for positive ones. Laying the groundwork for a change of this magnitude would take time. I'd have to be disciplined and roll with the punches.

And so, I began.

I imagined my brain as a childlike drawing of buzzing synapses, all linked like the branches of a tree. I imagined walking through the vast jungle in my mind, searching for and isolating the tree, locking into it and looking up into its branches and leaves to find the synapse that was sending out the rogue messages of Long Covid. I visualised snapping off the branch, and watching the new healthy shoots grow skyward. I imagined watering and feeding the healthy tree roots.

I also went deep into research mode. The Phosphatidyl Choline supplement was evidently helping my brain fog and as my thoughts became clearer, I was able to process more complex ideas, which in turn helped with the visualisations. I came to understand that when we learn a bad habit it takes over a map in our brains. Each time we repeat it, it reinforces the pattern, often becoming an obsession: unlearning is evidently significantly harder than learning. I needed to erase the 'bad' brain map blueprint, to weaken the connection. I learnt that I had 25,000 genes in my body, and reasoned that the vast majority of them must be functioning optimally. I could use my intention to reprogram my DNA and bring the faulty genes back into alignment. Knowing little of neurological science, I was out of my depth, with no guarantees of success. But putting my plan into practice gave me a renewed sense of hope; I felt empowered and energised.

As I became more confident, the visualisations and imagery became more complex. I was always in the present and focused on my vision, all other thoughts banished. Utterly determined, I repeatedly created a vision of what I longed for, carving out a new future for myself. I visualised running down the grey, painted wooden stairs at home with my spaniel jumping at my heels. In my mind I would rush out of the door, grabbing the lead on my way and running down the path inhaling the crisp, spring air. I painted a picture of enveloping myself in vibrant hues of lush greens and sky blues. I would run, hair flailing in the wind, feeling the earth and soil under my feet, past the apple blossom, through the park, smelling the cut grass. Dashing through the kissing gate, picking up speed. Together, the dog and I would race over the fields, squeeze past the split ancient tree and through the copse, stumbling over muddy tree roots into the wild meadow, pelting over to the tennis courts before turning the corner to head home.

I replayed this visualisation hundreds of times from my little room in my parents' flat. The poignancy and release of the homecoming often moved me to tears. I knew that the intensity of my feeling was significant, and helped to give greater clarity to my intention. I was opening my heart to teach my body what my future could look like. I became joyous and grateful for a future I was imagining for myself.

I discovered that my brain couldn't distinguish between physically performing the action and imagining it. The same area of my brain was being fired and I was creating positive plastic change in my neurons. Much like I had learnt a new language in my childhood, I realised that my brain had learnt Long Covid and I now had to *unlearn* it. My mind had been hardwiring the Covid relapses into my nervous system and I had been reinforcing the neural connection in my mind by revisiting the trauma over and over. I needed to become my own neurosurgeon; the new memories I created needed to be stronger than the old memories that were governing my preconditioned body.

In the days that followed, I added more powerful visualisations to my routine. I would imagine myself back in the squalid box room at home where I was first ill. Like a scene reminiscent of *Green Mile,* I would imagine the trauma and injury of Covid leaving my body like a black, poisonous cloud being ripped from my chest and expelled out through the open window and over the rooftops beyond. I would close my eyes and imagine pinning my shoulders back, standing forward on my tiptoes as if about to take flight, arms outstretched. I was consciously allowing the release of the suffering from my mind and body.

Taking deep breaths, I imagined a bright, healing light pouring in from the top of my head, into my head and neck, out into my arms and hands, down through my chest and tummy, into my pelvis and down my legs all the way to my toes. I visualised restoring all of my energy centres and filling every cell in my body. I listened to my pain with compassion and acceptance and told myself I no longer needed it. I concentrated on self-renewal. I visualised each part of my torso, my corpuscles, my blood stream, my muscle tissues, my gut, my immune and nervous system. I imagined all tension draining away and my heart beating naturally and healthily.

In this way, I became aware of every part of my body. Finally, I was paying attention.

It was one morning on waking that I realised my relapses had stopped. They had just faded away. I'd done it. I'd destroyed the repeating tapes in my head and changed the channel. I had erased the negative brain maps and grown new, healthy ones. I had downregulated the genes in my body that were making me ill and upregulated healthy ones.

The brain – the agent of my downfall – had been rewired.

Chapter 12

ANS Rewire

I had freed myself from the ghost of Covid but I still had a mountain to climb. Debilitating symptoms had put me in a wheelchair: excruciating pain in my back, neck, pelvis and in various points in my spine, plus a strange sensation in my elbows, as if they were dislodged and floating inside my skin. My pulse rate was higher than was healthy, my pounding heart a grim, frequent reminder.

Why was my body attacking itself from the inside? I couldn't understand it. Had Covid turned on a hereditary auto-immune disease? Even with my limited medical knowledge, I didn't think this was probable. I recalled the picture Dad had shown me of the rotated spine in the video. The skeletal and nervous systems were intrinsically linked. My nervous system must be affecting my spine – it made total sense.

The next morning I heard the familiar sound of Radio 4 flick on in my parents' bedroom. Within minutes, Dad was knocking excitedly at the door.

"Morning, Nic. How are you today? Well done, well done," he said, not waiting for my response. I could tell he was impatient to share something.

"Have you heard the news? Trump's got Covid!" he continued, a little too much excitement in his voice. "They're saying the next 48 hours will be critical; he's in a military hospital."

"He's not in great shape though, is he?" said Mum, following Dad in and smoothing down her dressing gown.

"No, he's in the high risk group for sure. Most of the White House will have it by now, it'll be rampant in there!"

"Oh Malc you do exaggerate, really," chided Mum.

"They'll all have it in there, Julie, I'm telling you! Mind if I switch on the news next door?" asked Dad, mindful of my self-imposed media blackout. I nodded.

"Would they postpone the election?" asked Mum.

"Not likely no, I don't think that's ever happened in U.S. history before, but I might be wrong," he said, logging on to fact check his own answer. "No never happened before," he confirmed, "Congress would have to pass a law to change the date. Crazy times, you really feel like this is living history, your grandchildren will be studying this at school in years to come!"

"I can imagine the schoolteachers now," I said, drily. "You'll be delighted to hear children, that we've added the Covid Years to the Plague and Spanish Flu for this term's topic of hideous historical diseases that ruined the lives of millions of people."

"You're sounding better," said Mum, "you're getting your sparkle back." She smiled. "There's a card come in the post for you, love." She put a brown envelope on my bed and went to put the kettle on.

I thumbed the ridge along the back of the envelope and ripped open the seam, recognising the handwriting of my friend, Lou. We were Long Covid buddies; she was still struggling with fatigue and loss of her sense of taste and smell.

Hi Nic,

I so hope you are improving? We miss you! I'm starting to feel a bit better, the fatigue is still there and the anosmia but I've been going to a treatment, a type of chiropractor, Lauren put me on to it. It's incredible, I really recommend you see Dr. Carter if you can?

Take care my love, we are thinking of you.

Love Lou

A pamphlet dropped out onto my bed.

Alive Chiropractic.

I glanced briefly at the blurb on the cover:

Network chiropractic care helps you relieve pain, revitalise your body, mind and spirit, and sustain a wellness lifestyle. A breakthrough clinical system called Network Spinal Analysis is at the core of this integrative whole-body approach. The power that made the body, heals the body.

I was dubious: I didn't like the term *wellness lifestyle* – what did it actually mean? It sounded too esoteric, but then I reminded myself that clinical knowledge had been of little use either. My experience of chiropractors was limited; I had never had a treatment, but friends and family members who struggled with bad backs would describe being twisted and cracked. The process sounded gruelling, painful and repetitive – there was no way my fragile body could cope with that kind of treatment. I was sceptical and the matter of cost also played on my mind. I'd been down so many health rabbit holes, tried numerous faddy diets, treatments and therapies… I couldn't cope with the emotional upheaval of another sham remedy.

I picked up my phone and noticed a new email from John. My brain fog had improved enough that I could read and comprehend correspondence for short periods, but mental work was still exhausting. I scanned his message to see what my next move should be. Recovery felt like playing a macabre game of chess, where any wrong move could mean death or permanent disability, yet where the rules of the game are unknown. I had to be precise and calculated, even while playing blind.

Dear Nicola

I am pleased to hear you are slowly improving. Your gut health and the transmission of messages to and from the brain via the vagus nerve is, I believe, at the root of all this, something we discussed from the very start. You should most definitely continue with your visualisation methods because they do work, there is a strong element of the mind in spontaneous remissions. It seems likely that a combination of poor gut health pre Covid and the infection have devastated your microbiome. As you now know, poor gut health can cause palpitations; gut health and heart health are intricately linked.

Firstly, the L-Glutamine you are taking is important for healing the gut and reducing the inflammation so keep that up. Secondly, eat onion soup regularly (proper stuff, not usual rubbish). Thirdly, all of the following are particularly beneficial for the gut: asparagus, garlic, onions, bananas, chicory, Jerusalem artichokes, avocado, leafy greens, fermented foods (e.g. sauerkraut) and lean proteins (make sure you take the digestive support of the Betaine Hydrochloric acid to bring your stomach acid up to where it needs to be). Disruption to the autonomic nervous system as you've experienced can result in a change to the metabolic secretions of your digestive enzymes, we need to get these back on track.

A really good probiotic supplement should help but it can easily be a big waste of money. The problem is, there are trillions of different organisms in the gut, most of which are never discussed. Certain strains can support numerous others and some strains can wipe out just as many if they get a chance!

So for now, I suggest spore-based probiotics which have far more chance of working and you test extremely low on 3 of the 5 main strains. Normal value is +8, you are -7 or -9 for Bacillus Indicus, Bacillus Clausii and Bacillus Coagulans. You are +7 for Bacillus Licheniformis and Enterococcus so near enough for those.

These strains are particularly good at revitalising others. It is possible they may need food, i.e. prebiotics but if you can eat some of the foods above it may not be necessary, at least not for now.

We have a serious nutritional problem in the UK and many other parts of the world and sadly the people who need things sorting most are often those least able to afford it. All I can do is try to help. You have at least made some good progress and that clearly wasn't the case for the first six months previously. I wish you all the best with your recovery.

I am always here if you need to speak on the phone.

All the best

John

I knew he was signing off. He'd given me all the help he could and I couldn't rely on his support forever. He'd already given so much of his time and asked for nothing in return. But I was terrified at being left without his help. Having researched as much as I could, there was very little left in my arsenal. How was I going to address my remaining health problems? I was at another crossroads and didn't know which way to turn. I also knew that I had to take responsibility for my own health. I was deeply unsure about the chiropractor treatment, but also knew I was playing the last card. This also terrified me, but doing nothing was not an option; insomnia was preventing my body from healing and the pains in my neck and spine were excruciating. I was still getting worse, critically so. I'd recently seen images of a previously healthy A&E doctor now resigned to walking with two sticks – a life cruelly limited by Long Covid.

That was not going to be me. I picked up the phone and booked an appointment.

Five days later, I struggled the few steps from the car into the waiting room. The receptionist mouthed a warm hello, wrinkled her nose and winked at me from behind her black-rimmed glasses. The room smelt fragrant and seemed to be pulsating with positive energy – a far cry from the sterile consulting rooms I was used to. Between chatting to clients, she hummed to herself as she tapped away on her computer. She smiled often and seemed genuinely happy. The atmosphere was warm and relaxed, almost joyous – a world away from the fear and trepidation unfolding outside.

Presently, a door clicked ajar, and Dr. Carter called my name. As she beckoned me through to her treatment room, her smiling eyes expressed a deep empathy and kindness. She seemed deeply grounded, wise, gentle, almost ethereal. I felt inexplicably drawn to her, like a wounded animal in search of shelter.

I took my seat as she glanced through my notes. Anatomical life size models of the spine and pelvis lay half hidden in alcoves, along with cushions and blankets. I could hear a diffuser whirring by the window.

"I'm Dr. Carter, but you can call me Daniella." She exuded a peace that I'd never noticed before in conversation with another person. "Tell me about your illness."

"I feel like I have anxiety, but it's strange… I don't feel anxious in my mind, it feels like it's in my body. I know this because when I do meditations for anxiety, I feel slightly better. I have brain fog, I'm barely sleeping. I've been having relapses, my body twitches, my coccyx feels like a tail between my legs, I have numb hands, palpitations on any exertion, I can't rotate my neck, I've pains in my chest and pelvis, I feel like I'm having a heart attack, I'm totally desperate... I need help."

I was gone then, sobbing deep, tearful guttural cries. I'd been knocked back so many times, told that I was imagining my symptoms, or that there was nothing that could be done for me, or that the virus was novel and there was no cure, or that I just had to put life on hold and hope to get better. In that moment, I felt wretched, defenceless, and deeply vulnerable. Would she listen to me and understand? Would she validate what I was saying?

"Everyone who comes to me seems to cry," she said, smiling with compassion. She handed me a tissue. "We mustn't hold onto our feelings; we need to open up. Our nervous systems are deeply influenced by our emotions."

"I've seen so many doctors," I sobbed, "no one has been able to help me. The neurologist I saw told me I was having panic attacks; he suggested anti-depressants and sleeping tablets. I've thought I was dying many times, I had to move out of my home. I'm so glad I found you."

I surprised myself with these last words. I knew others that had seen her, but she hadn't treated me yet, she hadn't done anything at all other than speak. I couldn't explain it but I felt I was talking to a healer. Relief flooded my body; I knew I could trust her.

She tutted gently at my story.

"I'm afraid many doctors are completely out of their depth, but they won't accept that they don't have all the answers. There are many people like you out there – people are starting to realise now."

"Network spinal analysis will help your body recover," she continued. "We must be patient though, because we are asking the nervous system to rewire, and it needs to understand what we are asking of it. Reprogramming it will take a while. We are essentially helping the body to send coordinated messages down the spinal cord.

"Your body is out of balance; when we experience stress, even though the trauma may not be present right now, it leaves its mark on the nervous system. The stress may be over and we are out of danger, but our nervous system doesn't know this and is stuck in the past. I expect you've been feeling helpless, and helplessness in the face of a perceived threat can be a strong trigger for biological stress responses.

"The effects of a trauma can stay with us long after the original shock, and they can be felt at a cellular level in our nervous systems. Conscious and unconscious memories can remain embedded in our bodies for years. The nervous system can fire up very quickly, but it often takes a long time to come back into alignment. Sometimes I can see the effects of traumatic births on adult spines.

"When you've been in a state of chronic spinal sympathetic activity for this long, the consequences can be severe. That's likely why you have palpitations – the pain you're feeling in your heart is the intercostal muscles contracting. I know it's frightening but you're not having a heart attack. It's a stress response."

I felt intense relief. She continued:

"The sympathetic state downregulates all functions that are not critical for survival, including healing and repair processes like the immune system. This causes other problems, because a suppressed immune system will allow pathogens in the gut and other areas. Sometimes you find past childhood illnesses re-emerge. A heightened and sustained state of anxiety will allow toxins to accumulate, contributing to fatigue and brain fog, because stress drains blood and oxygen supply from your frontal lobes.

"We need to give the nervous system the right information, and with a light touch to the right place, it will learn how to balance itself. In time you will become robust enough to deal with the stresses and strains of normal life. The three main factors that lead to stress are uncertainty, lack of information and loss of control. You've had all three over the last six months.

"Are you able to get up on the table?"

I nodded and gritted my teeth as I laboriously lifted my weak body onto the table. The effort caused my heart to hammer in my body. I tried not to visibly tremble. I felt deeply nauseous.

"Ah, you have curvature of the spine, we can fix that. Please move your head to the right… now to the centre… now the left, that's it." She touched my neck lightly with her finger before moving on to work on my feet.

"I can see you have rotation of your C1 and C2 vertebrae at the top of your spine," she said as she continued to work with light touches down my spine. "It only takes one negative thought to bring these out of alignment, and this affects your posture. The memory of a trauma can affect these vertebrae and when they are in the wrong place it affects blood flow to the brain; that might be why you feel you have brain fog. Now I would like you to consciously connect to your breath. Deep, long breaths please."

I breathed deeply, trying to ignore my heart protesting beneath my skin.

"Good. I can also see why you haven't been sleeping. Cortisol has stimulated your mind and body to stay awake and alert; high cortisol depresses melatonin. That's the hormone that helps you sleep. Meditation is good for dialling down stress and there are natural melatonin supplements you can take which may help – Amrita quicksilver liposomal melatonin is a good one. Your heart is working hard and will need extra magnesium. Copper also helps support the nervous system repair.

"I can also see from your spine that your appetite is poor.

Not surprising, because your body has been prioritising defence against a perceived threat, rather than hunger or digestion. We're working here to stimulate the vagus nerve to start the healing process; it will also improve the parts of the brain that support appetite regulation. The nerve needs to function properly in order to promote whole body health and to help regulate our emotions."

I nodded in acknowledgement, relieved to learn I'd been right to focus on restoring my vagus nerve function.

"The digestive tract is a sensory apparatus with a nervous system of its own. It's intimately connected to the brain's emotional centres and is vulnerable to emotional stress. You may find it takes a while for your symptoms to recede; your body will find the problem and work out how to heal it. Deep tension patterns will push their way out of your system which you might find uncomfortable, but they will subside.

"Okay Nic, you can sit up very slowly now, but please be gentle and kind to yourself. You've taken a big step today, your body may feel heavy. You'll need to drink plenty of water over the next couple of hours. The next time you come there will be others here; we call it entrainment. The idea is that mirror neurons fire in the brain when we see others having treatment; that will encourage your body to mimic the healing you see, and help shorten your recovery time."

I slowly got up. Sitting on the edge of the table, I rested my eyes on a watercolour of a bare-backed woman with a perfectly aligned spine while Dr. Carter held my forehead with one hand and gently manipulated my neck with the other. It felt like I'd received a deep tissue therapy all over my body. I was deeply relaxed and light-headed. Every nerve and cell tingled, as if they'd been awakened and were responding, regenerating.

I booked my next session for two days' time and clutching Dad's walking stick I headed haltingly out into the street and allowed myself a half smile. For the first time in many months I felt a new emotion: hope.

Chapter 13

The Dowser and the Gastroenterologist

The reprogramming of my nervous system was a success.

Within a few weeks, my insomnia was gone. That first night of eight hours' unbroken sleep was heavenly and I woke up smiling in disbelief. I was learning new tools daily, and slowly making headway. Climbing the stairs outside the flat was still a struggle, but I had more stability, more good days. I could now walk several laps around the flat and the muscle tone in my legs was improving. I was getting stronger.

Meditation, once my bête noire, had become my daily ritual. I had discovered Emotional Freedom Technique (EFT); as I tapped with two fingers as instructed in the meditation, all the trapped stress seemed to leave me. I found I could concentrate: if any rogue thoughts came up, I knew how to observe them and move on. I didn't berate myself for not being perfect; I wasn't a sage but with every day that passed, I was managing to quiet my mind little by little. Slowly I was transcending from distressed survival mode to a state of equilibrium, repair and renewal. I began to feel a sense of peace and wellbeing.

After meditating twice a day over several weeks, I found I

could regulate my emotions more easily and was more robust and resilient to living in the new, ever-changing world around me. Deep within my brain in the amygdala, fear circuits were dialling down; as with the visualisations, through meditations I was altering my neural circuitry. I was no longer triggered by bad news, nor startled by the doorbell. The violent warning of ambulance sirens no longer penetrated deep into my soul. I felt more patient and had a clarity of thought; my working memory improved and had regained access to rational thinking. My brain fog, which had been triggered by many factors including emotional reactions in my brain, had vanished. I began journaling.

I had set my intention to downregulate my body's stressors and upregulate the healing response. Free radicals left my body as I sent my brain the message it so desperately needed: that it could relax. Now I had given myself permission to heal, I was living in the present. My body began to come into alignment. I felt balanced and coherent. My heart rate calmed. My inflammation receded and the bumps on my skin began to fade. My hair had stopped falling out and felt thicker and healthier. I felt an inner peace I had never experienced as an adult, and I had a newfound joy for life.

I used the healing meditation to work on the areas of my body that needed healing: my pelvis and heels, elbows, my numb hands. Concentrating my intention on each area in turn, it truly felt as though my mind was instructing and committing my stem cells to repair damaged tissue.

Over the remaining days of November and into December, using guided healing meditations, I journeyed deep into my own mind, stepping outside of space and time. One time, an image came to me of what looked like a grey, withered, shadowy organ, part of my small intestine; it was ulcerated, pitted and cratered like the surface of the moon. Although initially confused by this anonymous shape, I felt strongly that it was the source of my vitamin B12 malabsorption. I visualised pink, fleshy skin healing, surrounded by a glowing diamond. I did this several times a day, imagining the B12 flooding my body and reaching all the tissues, organs and bones, not knowing how my body would heal, just believing that it could.

As I researched how to heal myself, I discovered that the specific meditation I was using prepared the body for healing by activating theta waves, the ideal mental and physiological state for healing. I also learnt that my brain was able to change quickly in meditation, repatterning neural pathways, suppressing bad genes and activating healthy ones. I had spent most of my adult life in high beta, fight-or-flight survival mode where healing comes last on the long list of essential functions. I discovered that stomach ulcers and digestive issues were often caused by chronic stress. In this context, my symptoms made sense.

I discovered many techniques to restore my body to homeostasis, the parasympathetic nervous system reset button that allows us to rest and digest. When my heart rate rose as cortisol rushed through my body on waking, I used deep, slow breathing, often accompanied by lavender essential oil behind my ear to bring my heartbeat back into equilibrium. I had subscribed to the vitalist philosophy: that the body has an innate intelligence to heal itself.

It had taken months to be referred to Gastroenterology and as the electric doors of the hospital swung open, I felt stronger than I had for many months. The doctor's gentle Irish lilt and compassionate demeanour put me at ease immediately. He was thorough and genuinely concerned for my welfare. I related my long clinical history; he checked my stomach carefully for anomalous signs of disease, and I was weighed by the nurse. Grabbing my tote bag, I gingerly pulled out the digestive supplements I was taking. I was concerned he might judge me, or tell me I was wasting my money but the opposite was the case. He reassured me that none of the supplements I was taking were harmful; rather, that they would be helping to repair my gut wall. He advised that the Gall Plus digestive enzyme would support my body to break down the food I was eating and I was relieved to hear him say that often a big hit of several B12 injections was enough to restore the body's B12 absorption function.

Having seen so many clinicians, diagnostic questioning had become second nature to me, but I felt more at ease than before. I was in a good place mentally and found myself telling my story from the perspective of gradual improvement rather than panicked desperation.

What he said next, amazed me.

He explained that my symptoms indicated I had a fungal infection in the gut that had compromised my immune system, likely due to a combination of Covid and compound stress. It was precisely the same diagnosis John had given me three months earlier through dowsing!

The doctor continued, explaining that intestines often

become ulcerated due to stress. These effects are generated by central nervous system pathways and hormones. An overproduction of cortisol was likely responsible for affecting almost every tissue in my body including the bones, and that stress could cause bone thinning effects if severe enough. My body had been acutely primed for action through the stress response for months, and that stored energy needed to be urgently mobilised or it would lead to disease. I wriggled my heels and felt the dull ache in my Achilles; the effects of cortisol overproduction had made themselves known all over my body.

It was extraordinary to hear John's diagnosis echoed back in this way. I was aware of the placebo effect, that maybe the supplements I was taking had made me *think* I was getting better and I therefore consequently recovered, or, an argument could have been made to the effect that I would have recovered at that point anyway. I would strongly dispute that given how ill I was – and how would you explain an accurate diagnosis by dowsing with no clinical information or examinations whatsoever, not even ever meeting me in person, simply chatting on the phone to me about my favourite holiday destinations? The concept is beyond logical explanation.

After three months I was still confounded by dowsing and my rational mind wanted to make sense of it. I imagined the default position of some would be that there was no evidence for it. A year ago, I would have been one of those doubters myself, but this was real and it certainly happened to me. Others had proffered me the more dismissive and patronising *whatever works for you* mantra but I was the empirical evidence, the living proof and I knew how ill I'd been. My recovery and the speed at which I was able to heal sufficiently to get out of bed was nothing short of miraculous. I reasoned that dowsing must be connecting either to a god of sorts, a higher power, a source, or a repository of universal truths – a global library of organised intelligence existing outside of the conscious mind that holds information on everything and everyone. The implications of the impact of dowsing on my recovery and subsequent diagnosis were at an existential level too abstract to comprehend or analyse at that point in my healing journey. I knew that roughly 85 percent of the mass of the universe is known as dark matter, made up of a material unobserved and unknown to scientists. Maybe dowsing is connected to dark matter and the quantum field. One thing I did know: there is so much we don't know.

Chapter 14

The Key

It was clear that for me Long Covid was the result of compound issues of the gut, nervous system and brain generated by the acute disease and exacerbated by chronic stress and a sustained fight-or-flight response that would not equalise. My compromised digestive system had been host to yeast infections that had allowed toxins to travel out of the gut wall and flood my immune system.

I had experienced the debilitating effects of stress at its worst; I was embodying the science of psychoneuroimmunology – my thoughts had become my reality. My trauma was in part the cause of my ill health. The fear and sense of sustained personal threat beyond my conscious awareness had clouded my rational thinking and flushed my body with poisons – cortisol and adrenaline, which destroyed tissues, caused inflammation, raised my blood pressure and weakened my heart and immune system.

My subconscious mind had taken a snapshot of the intense physical and mental trauma; past and present had become blurred. There was no ongoing existential threat but my body could not differentiate between actual and remembered physical stress; I was mentally replaying the trauma of survival based on harrowing memories, keeping a chemical record. I had inadvertently created the ultimate mind body connection – my thoughts were making me sick. This self-sabotage mindset compromised my ability to regenerate and heal. I had been infected by two viruses, one more dangerous than the other: the pandemic of fear.

Repetitive, scarring flashbacks of my trauma had been generating the illness that plagued me. Transformation could only occur from within. My damaged neural pain maps had been firing incessant warning signals, encouraging me to believe my issues were in my body when in fact, they were in my brain.

The human body has the capacity to heal naturally, so I could alter the genes that were misfiring. I just had to tap into that and be patient while the lasting change manifested.

I could not imagine or foresee how many future lockdowns, infections or mutant strains the country would have to endure in the coming months, but I myself had pursued a zero Covid policy. Covid was over for me. It had been eradicated in my mind and at a cellular level. There were no more mutations, no transmission and no more disease. There was no more panic or hysteria and no more fear. My world was no longer unsafe or hostile and I no longer feared the box room. I had freed myself from the tyranny of unconscious stressful and limiting beliefs. With the incredible support of my family, I had found balance and the cure within. The strength of my relationships had helped determine the force and speed of my recovery, and I was now able to do what the meditation had asked of me:

to connect to gratitude. No longer afraid of dying, I was only afraid of not fully living.

I had learned many lessons from my chronic illness: about life, what I valued, about myself. I learnt that I was resilient, determined, and stronger than I had previously given myself credit for. I had not previously recognised in myself what was possible, what had been there all along: a profound strength just waiting to be called upon. I held a bottomless reservoir for growth within, but could not learn and grow without enduring the struggle and pain first. I learnt I could control my physiology and biology by balancing my thoughts and emotions. I could prune the ecosystem of my mind and direct the new shoots towards health. I learnt there is no time to waste. I was no longer the same person I was a year ago. Within twelve months my skin had regenerated twelve times and 60 billion cells had been replaced in my body every day. I loved the new skin I was in.

I looked around my parents' sunny spare room one last time. The trusty supplement table cleared of tablets, the French doors that framed views of the hills, the room that had nurtured me and been my haven of security for eight long weeks. Empty now of all my belongings, it was no longer my ward room. The bed was stripped, my bag packed, and I was just a daughter visiting her parents again. I looked at my children's faces framed in glass on the shelf and knew I would shortly be with them; I could touch and hug them in the flesh. I longed to become their mum again and felt profoundly grateful to have that second chance.

I took one final glance through the frosty window at winter's day shadows cast over the garden; the icy shards of grass glistening in the raw sunshine, cow parsley seed heads frozen in time against an azure sky and hellebores already shifting their alignment in anticipation of the next dawn. As I watched a robin pecking repeatedly for the tiniest speck of sustenance from the near impenetrable earth, I marvelled at how in nature, nothing is wasted. Roots are hidden, primed and always waiting for growth under the surface; regeneration is always only a season away.

As I looked beyond the garden towards the hills, I turned inward, my mind taking me back to the dark, circular room one last time. Focusing on the locked doors, I breathed deeply. This time I was calm and composed, I knew what to do. I reached into the inside pocket of my jacket, hearing the faint clink of my ring as I clasped the metal key. With gratitude I got up off my knees and felt my way to the nearest door. Key turning smoothly in the lock, I grasped the door handle and pulled with both hands. The door swung open towards me. I stepped out towards the bright sky and ran into the open arms of my smiling family waiting for me on the other side.

The Drum

My hands cracked and bleeding, block out the light
I shiver as the drum signals your return. Fight or Flight.
The waves break over me, down and down we wrestle into the black.
The iron lung dredged from the deep
Terror comes, alone I must hit back

Rasping, the wretched night wanes.
My heart cracked and bleeding
Fearing shadows I swim on breathing
I weep, hot and swift they fall
Mindful now, I kick for shore

Laboured, we breathe through negative pressure
Clutching rainbows, you listen as we beat our drums apart,
Together in thanks
Shadows fall behind, and we unite
To walk the long road to conscious healing.

Afterword

I wrote the chapters in this book in March 2021, several months after I had recovered. When I read them now, I'm struck by how much has changed.

Although my symptoms have nearly all subsided, I am still left with residual peripheral neuropathy in my hands, which seems to coincide with my cycle. In fact, this morning I woke up with numbness in my left hand. Besides this, I have moved on from my illness, and from Covid.

I remember feeling so disappointed when my antibody test came back negative. I felt like I'd gone through a horrendous illness for nothing. And yet, I've only ever had Covid once, on that fateful day, 20th March, 2020. How come?

Immunity is not just about antibodies, it's about T cell response, too. I don't think this gets nearly enough attention. My T cells are robust and have prevented me from getting Covid again – something for which I am deeply grateful.

My illness taught me that the body is innately wise. Most of us do not tap into its wisdom nearly enough. I think both medical professionals and laypeople alike need to explore that more. Certainly, it needs to be recognised and acknowledged.

In the UK, the National Health Service (NHS) is an ailing

behemoth in the final throes of collapse, but it is taboo to talk about it. Why? We urgently need an alternative: a healthcare system that is not prescriptive but instead treats the whole person. Conventional western medicine does not have all the answers, so we need an approach that includes multiple modalities and therapies, and that pays due attention to the gut microbiome and nutrition. I was shocked to learn that medics only study one module on nutrition, despite food being so fundamental to our health. The chronically ill understand this all too keenly.

Above all, I passionately believe we need to take back control of our own health and health sovereignty. To illustrate why, here's just one more story. In 2020 when first ill with Covid, I was feverishly researching the internet, trying to find information on how I could treat my symptoms. I came across a doctor in China who said he was prescribing hydroxychloroquine, an anti-viral with promising results. Straight away, I phoned a physiotherapist friend at a local hospital and asked her if she could obtain some for me. No, she said, because it had not been authorised. A meta-analysis of studies has shown that early treatment with this well-established, cheap medicine can lower risk from Covid by 65%.[1]

Ivermectin is another well-established medicine with an excellent safety record that study after study have shown to be effective in both the prevention and treatment of Covid. Despite the World Health Organisation listing it as one of the world's essential medicines, regulatory bodies refused to approve it on

---

1 https://c19hcq.org/meta.html

grounds of safety. For context, ivermectin is available over the counter in many countries and has a safety record superior to paracetamol. Why were we denied access to this award winning repurposed medicine?

I would have done anything to be able to access these medicines when I was ill. Of course, I can never truly know what difference it would have made, but there's a significant body of robust evidence to indicate that it could have prevented me – and thousands of others – from immense suffering. To understand what might have happened had we had access, it's worth looking at Uttar Pradesh in India. Home to 231 million people, this state engaged in a huge, coordinated program to distribute ivermectin for both prevention and treatment of Covid 19. The result? By September 2020, Uttar Pradesh had almost completely eradicated the disease.[2] I share the belief of many scientists and doctors that, had ivermectin been freely available and approved for use worldwide, we would not have had a global pandemic.

In March 2021, I joined a non-profit called World Council for Health (WCH), whose mission is to safeguard health freedom for the world. It is a joy and privilege to work for an organisation with the integrity and vision to help humanity find a better way forward. Every week, WCH shares sound, accessible information on health that is freely available on its website. This includes treatment guides for Covid, a spike protein detox guide, and

---

2 https://pierrekorymedicalmusings.com/p/the-miracle-not-heard-around-the

hundreds of presentations and articles on a wide range of health-related subjects in multiple languages. I've included this plus other helpful links in the Resources section.

WCH also works with various partner organisations supporting the vaccine injured – a group that is sadly growing by the day, and yet which is still largely ignored and gaslit by medical professionals, governments and society at large. There is support out there, and doctors are finding and developing ways to treat the complex symptoms that so often present with vaccine injury.

For the record, I have not had any of the Covid vaccines. Given what I know now, I would never take them, nor give them to my children. I'm not an anti-vaxxer, I'm an ex-vaxxer, and our numbers are growing. WCH has developed a set of principles to live by, informed by the insights shared by many health and sovereignty experts. The first principle is *Act in honour and do no harm.* Our governments and health regulatory agencies ignored the clear safety signals from the Covid vaccines, they would do well to abide by this principle.

Our health is too precious to place in the hands of those unduly influenced by politics or profit. We're told to trust the experts, but experts do not necessarily have the answers. It's up to us. We really can find out what's best for us and our families by doing our own research and listening to our body's wisdom. This is what allowed me to return to full health and I've since met hundreds who've been through similar experiences, too. It may seem like uncharted territory, but it's actually a well-trodden path - and one that ultimately benefits all. In the words of Lao Tzu:

If you want to awaken all of humanity, then awaken all of yourself. If you want to eliminate the suffering in the world, then eliminate all that is dark and negative in yourself. Truly, the greatest gift you have to give is that of your own self-transformation.

Wishing you health and happiness.

Nic, 16th October, 2023

A note about dowsing

John and I eventually met up in person a year after I recovered. I was still intrigued by dowsing and asked him how it works. He explained that he used my voice, name and address to 'lock on' to me and he needed my express permission in advance in order to do that. He also explained that when treating people, he never asks for the health history of the patient in advance as that leads to bias, whether conscious or unconscious. There is evidently so much more we need to understand about this largely unexplored healing modality. Can you imagine a future where dowsers worked hand in hand with allopathic doctors?

Following my recovery, I taught myself how to dowse. It took many months before I felt I was getting the right answers, but slowly I began to feel that I was making progress.

One dark night in November 2022 I was driving home from a night out and could see several missed calls on my phone. I arrived at the house to find a very worried family – our dog was missing. There was a storm coming and the weather had turned to driving rain. My husband had already searched nearby roads and the surrounding fields for several hours. I set about grabbing my full wet weather gear, a torch and umbrella and headed out the back door, leaving the gate ajar incase Monty our spaniel found his way home. I headed up the lane and walked the full perimeter of our neighbouring estate calling his name as I went. I went into the nearby fields and in the park, I walked up and down terraces and called for him amongst garages and up and down the main road. Nothing.

After 30 minutes, I returned home, sopping wet and sat down at the table. I breathed deeply and picked up my dowsing pendulum, wondering if it could help me locate him. It was nearly 11pm and soon it would be too late to keep looking. I didn't have much time.

I started by asking my usual questions: can I dowse for, may I dowse for, is it right and appropriate to dowse for...? I asked if he was alive – yes. I asked if he had been stolen – no. I asked if he was ill – to this I got a response that I defined as 'slightly'. I asked the pendulum several questions about where he was and managed to narrow down a location about a half a mile from the house.

I called my husband to tell him I thought Monty was in the local park. He protested wildly and said he had already walked around the park calling his name many times. I insisted, and we put on our raincoats again and went back out. Dowsing had indicated he was on the right hand side, by the chainlink fencing that bordered a local school. I had never known him go to this spot before. Along the perimeter fence was a thick, high hedge. I stopped halfway along where dowsing had indicated he was, and crawled in through the hedge. I peered through the chain link fence but saw nothing in the dark. Just then I felt something soft at my feet. I shone the torch down and there was my daft spaniel, sopping wet, shivering with cold and sheltering under the hedge, looking very pleased to see me! My husband and I were both stunned.

Resources

Support groups

- The ME Association: https://meassociation.org.uk/

Health organisations

- World Council for Health – A grassroots initiative that offers expert, independent information to empower everyone to take care of their health and wellbeing. Its website is full of great resources, including a Spike Protein Detox Guide: https://worldcouncilforhealth.org/resources/spike-protein-detox-guide/
- Front Line COVID-19 Critical Care Alliance (FLCCC) – A US-based organisation founded by critical care doctors that develops and publishes expert treatment protocols, including I-RECOVER, an at-home treatment guide for Long Covid. https://covid19criticalcare.com/

Vagus nerve stimulation

- How to Stimulate Your Vagus Nerve: https://tinyurl.com/ycxyj7yd
- How to Laugh Alone for Health and Happiness: https://tinyurl.com/3saf6t2h

Network Spinal Analysis

- https://epienergetics.com/welcome-networkspinal/

- https://www.youtube.com/@DonnyEpstein

Aromatherapy

- Restoring Adrenal Health with Essential Oils: https://tinyurl.com/5n6cp568

Tapping

- An Introduction to Tapping – https://tinyurl.com/yc7jdsb7
- The Tapping Solution app – https://www.thetappingsolution.com/

Meditation

- Meditation for Cellular Anxiety - https://tinyurl.com/4sj6p5t3

Breathwork

- Self Help Therapy for Breathing Pattern Disorders – https://tinyurl.com/3acwjp3x
- Buteyko Method – https://www.learnbuteykoonline.net/

Loss of smell and taste

- Abscent – https://abscent.org/
- Restore Your Smell and Taste Naturally – https://tinyurl.com/scnjmxyh

The Ivermectin story

- 'The Vast Graveyard of Ivermectin Lies', with Dr Pierre Kory and John O'Shea – https://tinyurl.com/mw745j8h
- 'Dear Andy' – https://tinyurl.com/36h5yfd9

Gut health

- Dr Eric Berg DC - Diversity of the Microbiome – https://tinyurl.com/2u357fv6

General health

- Dr Sarah Myhill, Naturopathic Physician. Her website is full of useful content – https://www.drmyhill.co.uk/

Visualisation

- Visualisation to Help with CFS Recovery – https://tinyurl.com/yctbxx3j

Bibliography

- *Accessing the Healing Power of the Vagus Nerve* – Stanley Rosenberg
- *You are the Placebo* – Dr Joe Dispenza
- *Mind to Matter* – Dawson Church
- *How Your Mind Can Heal Your Body* – David R. Hamilton
- *The Brain's Way of Healing* – Norman Doidge
- *The Brain That Changes Itself* – Norman Doidge
- *When The Body Says No* – Gabor Maté
- *Dowsing: The Ultimate Guide for the 21st Century* – Elizabeth Brown

Acknowledgments

Thank you to my favourite people, Tom, Lily and Ella who never gave up hope for my recovery. I love you all more than words can say.

Thank you to my amazing parents Malcolm and Julie Robinson who let me move into their flat, nursed me back to health and researched hours of online video and information when I was too poorly to read or watch.

Thank you to Trish Watts who helped me to understand my energy envelope in the early days and encouraged me to keep an energy diary.

Thank you to my wonderful editor Caroline Wijetunge, who believed and identified with my story, encouraged and believed in me from the beginning, and carefully and skilfully edited the pages with wisdom, patience and care. I firmly believe universe meant for us to collaborate on this book.

Thank you to the talented artist James Nunn, who let me bore him on many dog walks telling my Covid story, understood the concept immediately and brought the book to life with his beautiful illustration. It was brilliant to collaborate with you.

To my friend Mel who introduced me to the world of integrative medicine and has been a joy to know for more than 30 years, two owls in a tree!

To Jane Sturmheit who pressed hard for John to treat me, despite being unwell herself.

To John Bradley, an incredibly knowledgeable, talented and

accurate dowser, you saved my life twice and never asked for anything in return. Thank you.

To my friends Sally and Lou who supported me during the fog of the lockdown and Lou who introduced me to network spinal analysis. I will be forever grateful.

To Ana Bold, who stepped in to help clean, cook and iron and support the kids when I had to leave home. Ana you are a truly special person and I am blessed to know you.

To Dr Daniella Carter, one of the truly good doctors. Your treatment is life restoring and vital. You have healed many thousands of people. Thank you for putting so many before yourself and for restoring my nervous system.

Thank you to my wonderful colleagues at World Council for Health, a dedicated and heart centred family, who constantly strive for a better way for a better world. I am proud to work with you.